W9-CAF-360

Stop Procrastinating

Understand Why You
Procrastinate—and Kick
the Habit Forever!

Frank J. Bruno, Ph.D.

Macmillan • USA

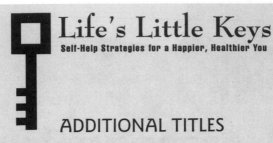

Life's Little Keys
Self-Help Strategies for a Happier, Healthier You

ADDITIONAL TITLES

Stop Worrying

Conquer Shyness

Defeat Depression

Conquer Loneliness

Get a Good Night's Sleep

*To those who struggle
with the problem of procrastination*

Macmillan General Reference
A Simon & Schuster Macmillan Company
1633 Broadway
New York, NY 10019-6785

An Arco Book

MACMILLAN is a registered trademark of Macmillan, Inc.
ARCO is a registered trademark of Prentice-Hall, Inc.

ISBN: 0-02-861302-3
Library of Congress Card Catalog Number: 96-085366

Manufactured in the United States of America

10 9 8 7 6 5 4 3 2 1

Cover design by Kevin Hanek
Book design by Scott Meola

CONTENTS

PREFACE

Procrastination is both distressing and corrosive. It is an acid that eats away at the quality of life, undermining everything in it from motivation to self-esteem.

You can obtain a vivid preview of the high cost of procrastination by turning to chapter 1 and reading the summary of Franz Kafka's short story "Before the Law."

Procrastination is not, of course, something that happens to you. It is not forced upon you by external circumstances. Instead, it is something that you *do*. It is a behavioral process. As such, it is potentially under the control of your intelligence and creative will.

Assuming that procrastination is one of your personal problems, can this book really help you overcome it?

The answer is yes.

Stop Procrastinating will reveal clearly:

1. Why you procrastinate.

2. How you can cope effectively with your own self defeating procrastination tendencies.

ACKNOWLEDGMENTS

A number of people have helped me make *Stop Procrastinating* a reality. My thanks are expressed to:

Barbara Gilson, senior editor at Macmillan, for her recognition of the value of the book and for being a supportive and creative editor.

Jennifer Perillo, editor at Macmillan, for her assistance and for her appreciation of the book's themes.

George J. McKeon, artist, for his capturing of key ideas in cartoon form.

Bert Holtje, my agent, for encouraging the development of the book.

My wife, Jeanne, for our many meaningful discussions.

My son, Franklin, for our conversations about language and meaning.

George K. Zaharoupoulos, a true teaching colleague, for his steadfast encouragement of my writing projects.

1 THE "I'LL-DO-IT-TOMORROW" SYNDROME: MISSING OUT WHEN OPPORTUNITY KNOCKS

If you have a tendency to procrastinate, you are not alone.

Procrastination is a problem as familiar as the common cold. Who does not know what it is to procrastinate? Who has not put off a chore for a future date?

More than once I have surveyed either an audience or a college class, giving these instructions: "Make a short written list of your bad habits. Add a brief comment after each."

Fully 60 percent of the individuals who respond include procrastination on the list.

Here are some examples of comments I have received:

1. "I have goals, plans, and dreams that I never reach. Unfortunately, I'm a dreamer, not a doer."

2. "I just can't seem to get things done around the house. There are sprinklers to repair, books to organize, closets to clean out, and everything just sits there while I wonder where to start."

3. "I put off studying for an examination until the last minute, then I burn the midnight oil cramming. I get Cs when I should be getting As."

4. "My husband and I want to travel, but somehow we just never get around to it."

5. "I want to lose weight, but I keep putting off going on a diet."

6. "I need to go shopping for an outfit for my sister's wedding. It's only a week away and I don't have any idea what I'm going to wear."

7. "I haven't written a letter or called my brother in over three months. Every day I think about it, and every day I don't do it."

8. "Someday I'm going to stop smoking, and someday ain't coming around for some reason."

9. "There is someone I work with that I want to ask out on a date. I've got a crush. I've been mooning over this person for about three months, but can't seem to act intelligently on my feelings. I hope she doesn't get away while I'm waiting."

If procrastination is undermining the quality of your life, you will find that this book offers practical suggestions that will help you put a stop to the tendency.

Kinds of Procrastination

Procrastination is not just one big bad habit. It is possible to look at various aspects of procrastination, to identify kinds of procrastination. The analytical process of dividing procrastination into parts will help you come to grips with your own behavioral tendencies.

Here are the principal kinds of procrastination:

1. *Functional Procrastination.* One of the meanings of procrastination is simply "to defer or postpone." There are certainly times when it is appropriate and correct to defer or postpone an action. Perhaps you are *really* not feeling well. Or maybe

some other activity has a higher priority. Maybe you haven't gathered enough information yet. Just because you procrastinate doesn't mean you're being irresponsible, lazy, or inattentive.

2. *Dysfunctional Procrastination.* This is procrastination that is useless. As a result of this kind of procrastination, important tasks remain undone. Opportunities are missed. Challenges are avoided. Important goals and dreams are not realized. Dysfunctional procrastination is self-defeating.

   As one woman in her forties said, "I look back on my life and think about what I might have done, what I might have been. And it makes me feel angry with the foolish person I was."

3. *Short-term Procrastination.* You have either a target time or a target day, and you don't make an early enough start.

   The words *short term* can apply to a few hours or a few days depending on the target day. You need to dress for a special occasion, and want to leave your home at 6 P.M. It is short-term procrastination if you don't start dressing until 5:45.

   You need to study for an important examination. The date is Wednesday, November 8. The instructor gave you two weeks to make preparations. If you don't study until two days before the test, this is short-term procrastination.

4. *Long-term Procrastination.* You have some big goals and large dreams. You are going to start a business. You plan to go to college. You think about entering a profession. You want to travel to far away places. You want to write a novel. You want to design your own home and build it. You want to learn to fly an airplane. But here you are. Years have gone by and you haven't made any real start toward actually achieving your goals and dreams.

5. *Chronic Procrastination.* This is procrastination that has become a habit. It is persistent, it is a problem, and it is something that you have been living with for quite a while. More correctly, the complete term is *chronic dysfunctional procrastination*, implying that it is both a nagging problem and a self-defeating one. For the sake of brevity, when the term *chronic procrastination* is used in this book, it implies the notion that the behavior is also dysfunctional.

It is chronic procrastination that is our prime consideration in the pages to come. Chronic procrastination is a thief. It steals your time and it robs you of the satisfaction that you might enjoy as a result of important accomplishments.

Helping you discover practical ways to stop chronic procrastination is the main goal of this book. However, other kinds of procrastination will be considered as we go along.

The Goof-Off

It is easy to imagine a movie entitled *The Goof-Off*. The protagonist could be either a male or a female, depending on the actual script. The part should be played by an actor with both dramatic and comedic talents such as Steve Martin or Lily Tomlin. In the end the central character wins the boy or the girl by luck, not by intelligent effort. We as members of the audience would get a lot of laughs out of the goof-off's waste of time and foul-ups. We often laugh at another person's shortcomings. Perhaps this is because we see our own traits in exaggerated form, as in a fun-house mirror.

Yes, chronic dysfunctional procrastination might make the basis for a very funny story. But it is only funny from the outside. From the inside, there is nothing funny about fouling up and losing. As the philosopher Voltaire said, "Life is a comedy to those who think, a tragedy to those who feel." If the goof-off in the story were to really be a living, breathing person like you or me, there would be emotional pain involved.

And the ending of such a film would be unrealistic. In life itself we generally don't find the right person because chance happens to smile on us in a whimsical way.

No, in the end there's really nothing funny or amusing about failure. The waste of time is just that, a *waste*.

The Time Machine

Easily H. G. Wells's most popular novel was *The Time Machine*. The hero voyages into the far future and finds out that humankind has made a mess out of things. But the real fascination of the novel is in neither its plot nor its writing. The attraction comes from the subject itself, the idea of *voyaging in time*. We are fascinated by time, and hardly understand what it is. Wells, borrowing from Einstein's Special Theory of Relativity, said that time is the fourth dimension. (The other three are height, width, and length.) Time is the fourth dimension because you don't really know *where* something is in space until you know *when* it's there.

One of my standard dictionaries lists twenty-five definitions of time. Apparently, it is a very difficult concept to define.

Or is it? It can be argued that we all know intuitively what time is. God or Nature gives us the basic idea at birth. This was the view of the philosopher Immanuel Kant. Even infants seem to know that Event A precedes Event B. Preschoolers certainly have no problem understanding that breakfast comes before lunch. And when they are eating lunch, they remember eating breakfast. So there is no problem. They both understand and use time in their thinking.

From our point of view let's think of time as a kind of gift, the very substance of our lives. A gift should never be discounted in importance just because it came to you without effort, just because it *is* a gift. On the contrary, it is important for us to recognize time as the precious gift it is. Imagine yourself receiving a diagnosis from a physician stating that you have a fatal terminal illness. A natural question is to ask, "How much longer do I have, doctor?" Your first concern is for the amount of *time* that remains.

If you or I are fortunate enough to live out an average human life span, according to the National Center for Health, we will live almost 74 years. That's approximately 27,000 days. It's a lot of days. But not so many that you can afford to take a wasteful attitude toward them. Every day is precious in its own way. And I'm not talking about work and objective accomplishments only. The wise use of time allows us to work, love, and play in balanced proportions.

Some people speak of "killing the day" or "killing time." What a dismal way to talk and think. Instead we want to speak of "using the day" or "enjoying the day." This is the optimal mental attitude.

By the way, our prognosis is somewhat better than the above statistics suggest. The 74-year figure is life expectancy at birth. If you are older, believe it or not, your total life expectancy goes up! This is because at any given age you have picked up the statistical expectancy of people who have died before you. Consequently, if you are 25 years old, your remaining expectancy is 51 years, making a total of 76 years. If you are 50 years old, your remaining expectancy is 28 years, making a total expectancy of 78 years. Even if you are 75 years old, and over the life expectancy at birth, you have a remaining expectancy. It is 10 years, making a total expectancy of 85 years.

I tell you this because I *do* want you to think of yourself as rich with future, as having enough "world and time." Nonetheless, your days and mine are numbered. We should spend time wisely.

Counseling Experiences

I have spent quite a few years of my life working as a psychology instructor, psychotherapist, and counselor. The knowledge I have acquired from both my own personal experiences and my interactions with others are passed on to you in this book in the form of tips and practical suggestions. These are self-directed coping strategies, and they work.

If there is one thing I have learned, it is that sometimes relatively small changes make for big results. Consequently, my approach to both therapy and self-help is oriented toward the present and things you can actually do to help yourself.

Instead of thinking in terms of your personality, and believing that something is wrong with it, think in terms of your conscious thoughts and your behavior. These are accessible to you, and you can change them.

It is not useful to say to yourself, "I am a procrastinator." This makes procrastination a personality trait, and suggests that it is a part of your being. The two words *I am* weld you and procrastination into an identity. You need to disidentify from procrastination. Consequently, it is useful to say to yourself, "I procrastinate more than I want to, and I'm going to do something about it." Now procrastination becomes a behavior, not a personality trait. And you can change a behavior.

Tomorrow

Tomorrow. It's a friendly word somehow. You can always do it tomorrow. Little Orphan Annie in the musical version of her life, *Annie,* sang that she loved tomorrow because it was always a day away. And, of course, tomorrow will be better than today.

But tomorrow can be an unfriendly word too. By relying too much on tomorrow you can rob today of its own special and unique character. Take a look at today. Today is the only day you can actually do anything. You can't undo the past. You can atone for something you feel guilty about, but you can't undo it. You can't undo unhappy childhood experiences, but you can choose the attitude you take toward them in the present.

And you can't actually *do* anything in the future. We say, "I'll do it tomorrow." But when tomorrow comes it is another *today*." And you have to do it, whatever "it" is, right here in the present.

A tendency toward chronic procrastination involves the mental habit of looking too much toward tomorrow as a better day to actually *do* something than today is. As the title of this chapter indicates, problem procrastination of this type can be called the "I'll-Do-It-Tomorrow" syndrome. A syndrome is a constellation of signs and symptoms. Take a look at the list below and check off how many of the items you agree with. The more items you check, the more you are making yourself a victim of the syndrome.

Checklist for the "I'll-Do-It-Tomorrow" Syndrome

1. I don't like to start a project until I have all of the information I need.

2. I want to travel, but I'm not sure where or when.

3. I want to meet new people and make new friends, but don't know where to start.

4. Someday I want to improve my professional or vocational status by getting more education.

5. I have an important project, a pretty big one, that I'm waiting to work on until I've got a good-sized block of time available for it.

6. I'm going to lose weight (or stop smoking, or stop drinking, or stop abusing drugs) when there is less pressure on me.

7. When things ease up a little and I'm not run so ragged by so many things, I'm going to show my partner more love and affection.

8. I'm going to get my clothes (or my books, or my files, or the things in the garage) organized one of these days.

9. If I have an unpleasant chore to do or a difficult task to accomplish, I am likely to put off doing whatever it may be until the last minute.

10. I generally leave my home late, not allowing myself enough travel time to get to work, a date, a party, or some other event that is associated with a relatively punctual arrival.

When Opportunity Knocks

One of the ideas held by persons who suffer from chronic procrastination is that opportunity knocks for others, but not for them. They fail to see that opportunity may be overlooked and not acted upon because of procrastination. There are few things sadder than missing out when opportunity knocks. "Before the Law," a story written by the Austrian author Franz Kafka, makes this point effectively. The story is summarized below. Keep in mind that Kafka's writings were fantastic and dreamlike.

A young man is traveling from his homeland to a better place (another world or land called *the Law*). Early on his journey he encounters a door and a doorkeeper. The door is open. He begins to go toward the door, but the doorkeeper sternly says, "Wait!"

"Wait for what?" asks the voyager.

"Just wait."

"Why?"

"I said just wait." The doorkeeper provides a stool. "Sit here."

The young man sits down. Minutes pass. Hours pass. The doorkeeper gives no sign that the young man can come forward. Finally, the man stands and walks toward the doorkeeper. "Can I go through now?"

"No."

"But why not?"

"Just go sit down."

The youth goes back to the stool. He waits for hours and then for days. He asks from time to time if he can go through the door, but the answer is always no. The days turn into months. The months turn into years. The youth becomes middle aged, then old and gray. He no longer

≋   ≋   ≋

asks if he can go through the door. He just stares at it, waiting for a sign from the gatekeeper.

When the now-old voyager is about to die he asks the doorkeeper, "How does it come about that in all these years no one has come seeking admittance but me?"

The doorkeeper answers, "No one but you could gain admittance through this door, since this door was intended only for you. I am now going to shut it."

≋ ≋ ≋ ≋ ≋ ≋ ≋ ≋ ≋

What do you make out of this story? I won't try to overanalyze it for you because, as I said, it has a fantastic dreamlike quality. Enrich it by projecting your own meanings on it. However, to my own mind it seems that the story compellingly gets across the point that we are often blind to opportunity. It also makes the point that we foolishly let an outside factor (the doorkeeper) stop us when that factor has no real right or authority to do so. The protagonist of the story only assumed that the doorkeeper had the power and right to stop him, and his assumption was in error.

The youth should have been audacious enough to have walked through the door. He should not have waited. And he might have eventually arrived at a better world.

But you don't have to make the mistake that he made.

The Last Word

This book can help you put a stop to chronic procrastination in two principal ways:

1. It will help you understand why you procrastinate.

2. It offers a number of self-directed practical suggestions that, if applied, will provide you with effective ways to stop procrastinating.

An English proverb says, "One of these days is none of these days." The application of the ideas in this book to your daily life will turn the one-of-these-days outlook into a satisfying do-it-today attitude.

Key Points to Remember

□— Procrastination is as familiar as the common cold. Fully 60 percent of individuals I have

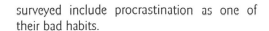

surveyed include procrastination as one of their bad habits.

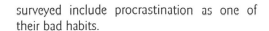 Functional procrastination is no problem. It takes place when there is a good reason to defer or postpone an action.

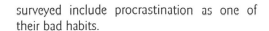 Dysfunctional procrastination is useless, resulting in important tasks remaining undone, opportunities missed, and a failure to realize important goals and dreams.

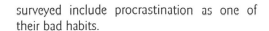 Chronic procrastination is procrastination that has become a habitual way of behaving.

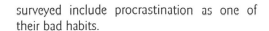 Although time in physics is a complex concept, even children appear to have an intuitive understanding of its meaning.

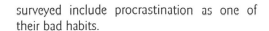 Time is a gift that should not be wasted. The notion of "killing time" is a dismal one.

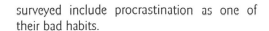 Although it is psychologically healthy to think of yourself as rich with future, it is also important to realize that our days are numbered.

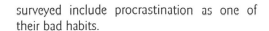 It is not useful to say to yourself, "I am a procrastinator." It *is* useful to say to yourself, "I procrastinate more than I want to. And I'm going to do something about it."

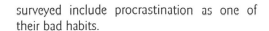 Relying too much on tomorrow robs today of its own special and unique character. Today is the only day in which you can actually do anything.

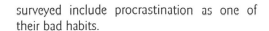 We are often blind to opportunity. We let an outside factor stop us when that factor has no real right or authority to do so.

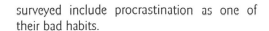 Keep in mind the English proverb that says, "One of these days is none of these days."

2 FATIGUE AND DELAY: HOW CAN YOU DO ANYTHING IF YOU DON'T HAVE ANY ENERGY?

Energy is a vital ingredient in every behavior. Without energy you can't do a thing, any more than a lightbulb can shine brightly from a flashlight containing weak batteries.

The primary reason we do anything at all is because of the biological drives: hunger, thirst, sex, sleep, the need to escape from pain, and so forth. These drives are sometimes called the energizers of behavior. In fact, take note of the word *drive* itself. It means something that makes you go, something that makes you move. It is instructive to note that another word for a corpse is a "stiff." A dead person is unmoving, stiff. Obviously, a deceased individual has no biological drives.

In order to have a high level of energy you must satisfy your body at an organic level. Otherwise you will always be waiting until a better time to do almost anything, a time when you will "feel better" or "have more energy."

Lack of energy, or chronic fatigue, is a common cause of procrastination. Consequently, if you find yourself procrastinating "all of the time," maybe you lack sufficient energy for work or recreation.

It is common to hear someone say:

"I'm out of gas."

"I'm so pooped I could pop."

"I'm burned out."

"I've had it! I can't lift another finger."

"I'm feeling rundown. Maybe I have iron-poor blood."

"I don't know. Lately I just can't get myself going. I feel tired all of the time."

"I'm exhausted."

Any of the above statements can serve as a basis for begging out of work to be done, a recreational outing, or even a sexual encounter. The plea is for more time, for a delay, in order for the fatigue to dissipate.

The relationship of energy to procrastination is a kind of chicken-and-the-egg problem. Do you procrastinate because you really don't have any energy? Or, are you using lack of energy as a rationalization for procrastination? The use of fatigue as a feeble excuse for procrastination will be discussed in chapter 4. However, let's now take fatigue at face value and assert that there are times when it is really true that you have a hard time doing things because you lack sufficient energy.

The biological basis for procrastination is not the principal theme of this book. On the contrary, all future chapters take a psychological approach. Nonetheless, having said this, it is also important to realize that energy is a *requirement* for action, just as a car needs a running motor with enough horsepower. On the other hand, the car won't go if it isn't put into gear. Other chapters discuss putting the "car" (yourself) into gear. This single chapter is devoted to making sure the car's motor has enough horsepower to go at all.

Fatigue

Chronic fatigue syndrome is a condition that has received publicity in recent years, and it is common to hear someone with a low energy level say, "I guess maybe I have

chronic fatigue syndrome." It's important to understand that this condition is not a well-defined illness such as diabetes or tuberculosis.

There is in fact an important distinction to be made among (1) chronic fatigue syndrome, (2) significant, persistent fatigue, and (3) everyday, garden-variety fatigue.

Chronic fatigue syndrome is more correctly called *chronic fatigue immune dysfunction syndrome.* A syndrome is a constellation of related signs and symptoms. The U.S. Center for Disease Control identifies these as the principal symptoms often associated with chronic fatigue syndrome: sensitive lymph nodes, disturbances in sleep patterns, nervous system problems, throat irritation, pains in the muscles and joints, slight fever, chills, general weakness, headaches, and, of course, fatigue. The cause or causes of the syndrome are not well defined or understood. However, a major hypothesis in the past, and one that is still useful to some extent, is that the syndrome arises in part due to the residual effects of the Epstein-Barr virus, the same virus that causes mononucleosis. Mononucleosis is the so-called "kissing disease" and is commonly contracted in adolescence and young adulthood.

Significant, persistent fatigue need not be associated with chronic fatigue syndrome. Significant fatigue can arise from many causes, including restriction of blood flow due to atherosclerosis, liver problems, a sluggish thyroid gland, a tendency toward hypoglycemia (low blood sugar), an adverse reaction to a drug, and diabetes.

If you appear to suffer from either chronic fatigue syndrome or significant, persistent fatigue, you should consult a physician.

Everyday, garden-variety fatigue is the kind of fatigue we all experience from time to time. We say, "I'm dragging," or, "I'm all worn out," or "I've had it!" Everyday fatigue should not be slighted and deemed unimportant even though it is not a clinical medical problem. Nonetheless, it can be an important causal factor in procrastination.

Boosting Your Energy Level

Below you will find some common-sense, practical tips for boosting your energy level. An adequate energy level will contribute to a genuine desire to "do it now" instead of tomorrow.

VITAMINS AND MINERALS

Be Sure You Have an Adequate Intake of Vitamins and Minerals. In theory you shouldn't have to take vitamin and mineral pills. If you really understand nutrition and eat in balanced proportions from the four basic food groups, perhaps you don't need supplements. However, it is obvious that a lot of us are undernourished, even people who are overweight. You can take in too many calories and be overfat, but that doesn't mean you are, in fact, well nourished.

Consider the way many of us eat today. It is common to eat on the run, to depend on fast foods and take-out items. Perhaps you don't eat enough green vegetables. Perhaps you don't like fruit. Maybe you eat french fries instead of baked potatoes. French fries are high in saturated fat and depleted of the vitamin C available in a baked potato. Food abuse is a large-scale problem. The first line of defense is to know what you are doing and to eat right.

As a second line of defense, it is probably a good idea to take a multiple vitamin on a daily basis. This will give you essential vitamins and minerals. However, don't become a vitamin pill faddist. It's not necessary. And, in fact, it is possible to take too much of certain vitamins, such as A, E, and D. Excessive intake can be toxic.

Going back to the first line of defense, how you eat, it is difficult to overdose on vitamins obtained in a natural way. Let's survey some of the key vitamins involved in maintaining a high energy level, and indicate their prime sources.

Vitamin C will help you fight off infections, and it has a beneficial effect on your immune system. A deficiency of this vitamin is definitely associated with fatigue and becoming tired too quickly. Also, shortness of breath is linked to a vitamin C deficiency. The following foods are excellent sources of vitamin C: oranges and other citrus fruits, peppers, tomatoes, berries, cauliflower, and green vegetables.

Vitamins in the B-complex family will help your body synthesize key neurotransmitters, chemical messengers that are important to a sense of well-being. And a sense of well-being is an important ingredient in being active and getting things done. Deficiencies in the B-complex family are associated not only with fatigue, but such adverse effects as apathy, confusion, sensitivity to light, and sleep disturbances.

There are eleven vitamins in the B-complex family, and it is beyond the scope of this book to provide details on each one. However, the sources of the vitamins overlap because they *are*, after all, a family. Consequently, I will focus on four members of the family and indicate their sources. If you see to it that you obtain high levels of the B vitamins indicated, it is quite likely that you will obtain enough of the whole complex Vitamin B_1, or thiamine, can be obtained readily in wheat germ, brewer's yeast, and bran. Whole grain bread is a good source of bran.

Niacin is an unnumbered member of the B-complex family. Excellent sources of niacin include peanuts, brewer's yeast, wheat germ, liver, beef, poultry, and fish.

Vitamin B_6, or pyridoxine, is particularly important because a deficiency of this vitamin is associated with low blood sugar, or hypoglycemia. Vitamin B_6 is available in a broad range of foods including whole grain bread, meat and fish, peanuts, walnuts, bananas and other fruits, avocados, and wheat germ.

Folic acid, or folacin folate, is an unnumbered member of the B-complex family. A deficiency of this vitamin is associated with a poorly functioning memory, feeling irritable, and sluggish thought processes. The principal natural source of folic acid is leafy green vegetables. If you eat a lot of your meals out and rely on a salad made from iceberg lettuce for folic acid, you are deceiving yourself. This kind of lettuce is *not* a good source of folic acid.

However, romaine lettuce, with its broad, dark green leaves, is.

Vitamin A promotes the building of new tissue in your body. This is an important factor in maintaining your energy level. A vitamin A deficiency is associated with the vague impression that you ache all over, tiredness, and headaches. Vitamin A is a fat-soluble vitamin, and it is possible to overdose on fat-soluble vitamins when too many supplements are taken. Symptoms of a toxic overdose include feeling cross and irritable, moodiness, a loss of appetite, and yellowing of the skin. It is probably a good idea to limit supplements to whatever you can obtain from a good multiple vitamin-mineral formula. Excellent natural sources of vitamin A include green leafy vegetables, carrots, fruits in general, and both beef and chicken liver.

Vitamin E is a vitamin of particular importance because it is an antioxidant. It may help slow down the aging process. Also, it assists in the formation of red blood cells. Red blood cells deliver oxygen to other cells, and this delivery system is of great importance in maintaining a high energy level. Like vitamin A, it is possible to take in too much supplemental vitamin E because it is a fat-soluble vitamin. The principal symptom of a toxic overdose is high blood pressure. Excellent natural sources of vitamin E include whole grain bread, oats, rice, peanuts, cabbage, spinach, asparagus, and broccoli.

FIBER

Be Sure That Your Diet Has Enough Fiber. Fiber comes in two forms: soluble and insoluble. Soluble fiber absorbs water and expands the same way in which a dry sponge absorbs water. Insoluble fiber neither absorbs nor expands. Both kinds of fiber are important in maintaining the movement of fecal matter through the gastrointestinal system. Constipation is a common complaint in our society, and over-the-counter laxatives account for a large percentage of pharmacy sales. Persons who suffer from chronic constipation complain that they are also "sluggish." Being "bound up" is associated with a lack of general vitality. In order to keep your general energy level up, it is important to avoid constipation.

One of the reasons that constipation is so common is because in our culture we tend to eat a *low-residue diet*, a diet inadequate in both kinds of fiber. Let's say that you eat a stack of pancakes, eggs, and bacon for breakfast. You have a hamburger, a milkshake, and french fries for lunch. Assuming that the pancakes and the hamburger buns are made with white flour, a common principal ingredient, you have so far obtained virtually no fiber in your diet. None of the foods indicated have any fiber worth talking about.

Our low-residue diet has been implicated as a leading cause of colon cancer. In underdeveloped countries where it is usual to eat a lot of fiber and smaller amounts of processed foods, colon cancer is less common.

Good sources of soluble fiber include oatmeal and all kinds of fruits. Good sources of insoluble fiber include whole grain breads and all kinds of vegetables. Soluble fiber has a gentle effect and provides bulk in your diet. Insoluble fiber acts like a whisk broom, sweeping particles out of little pouches in your colon.

If you don't get enough dietary fiber, you can readily supplement the fiber in your diet. One effective way to obtain more soluble fiber is to stir about one-eighth of a cup of psyllium in water every morning. Psyllium is readily available in natural form in health food stores. If you find natural psyllium unpalatable and somewhat hard to take, it is the principal ingredient in many palatable over-the-counter advertised products available in your local pharmacy.

One effective way to obtain more insoluble fiber is to add about one-quarter of a cup of all-bran cereal to your daily diet. If you like breakfast cereal, just combine all-bran with the other cereal. If not, eat the all-bran alone with a little milk.

MEALS

Eat Light Meals. If there is something you need to get done after you eat, it is better to eat a light meal. Let's say that you consume a heavy lunch. Too many calories of any kind, protein or carbohydrate, will result in a sluggish feeling. The process of digestion activates the para-sympathetic division of the autonomic nervous system and lowers central nervous system arousal. This means that you are less alert and less vigilant as blood is drained from your brain and diverted to your gastrointestinal tract.

Food is a natural tranquilizer, and too much of it at one time makes you feel dull and dopey. It is hard to see how a person who feels this way can accomplish much. If he or she does function, it is with effort. It's like dragging a sack of stones uphill.

One of the important ways to keep your energy level high all day is to be sure that breakfast and lunch are light. If you have important work to do after dinner, it should be light too.

SNACKS

Have Two Snacks a Day. If you find your energy decreasing between meals, a snack can be helpful. In fact evidence suggests that we are innately nibbling and snacking creatures rather than three-square-meals-a-day creatures. Consequently, snacking fits in well with the light-meal way of eating.

If you have breakfast at 7 A.M. and lunch at noon, around 9 or 10 A.M. is a good time for your first daily snack. If you have lunch at noon and dinner at 6 P.M., then around 3 or 4 is a good time for your second, and last, daily snack.

Here is a principal *don't* of snacking:

Don't have a snack that is high in refined sugar. Examples of such snacks include soft drinks, candy bars, doughnuts, and ice cream. If you are buying your snack in packaged form, read the caloric and carbohydrate content. It is easy to take in 200 or even 300 calories from a high sugar snack. This many calories will not give you a sustained energy boost.

Although it is true that a snack high in refined sugar will give you a short burst of energy by quickly raising your blood sugar, this is deceptive. The energy level will not be sustained, and your blood sugar will drop. And, combined with too many calories, this second negative factor will add to a sluggish feeling.

Obviously, many people are making a mistake by following the crowd and ingesting popular snacks that are readily available on conveniently placed counters and racks near cash registers.

Here is a principal *do* of snacking:

Do have a snack that is high in protein. Keep the calories down around 80 to 120. A high-protein snack will give you sustained energy. Foods high in protein are metabolized slowly and help to keep blood sugar at optimal levels. The fact that the calories are low will prevent the parasympathetic division of your autonomic nervous system from kicking in and making you drowsy.

Here is a list of low-carbohydrate/high-protein snacks that will meet the criteria indicated above:

1. One-quarter cup of almonds or peanuts.

2. A tablespoon of peanut butter.

3. A slice of gluten bread.

4. One-half cup of low-fat cottage cheese.

5. A hard-boiled egg.

6. A slice of low-fat American cheese.

7. A piece of broiled chicken without the skin.

8. One-quarter can of tuna or salmon.

9. A slice of boiled ham.

10. An eight-ounce glass of nonfat milk or a six-ounce glass of low-fat milk.

If you study the labels on containers, you can easily extend the list.

Peanut butter is high in fat, but this is no problem if you don't overdo its consumption. The important point to be made about peanut butter is that peanut oil in its natural form is a monounsaturated fat and is not likely to contribute to atherosclerosis, an important factor in strokes and heart disease. (The older, informal term for atherosclerosis is "hardening of the arteries.") However, when peanut butter is hydrogenated, it appears that the body treats it like a saturated fat (a fat that is solid at room temperature). Saturated fats are converted by the liver into cholesterol, and this in turn appears to contribute to atherosclerosis. So buy the kind of peanut butter you have to mix in order to distribute the oil. You can readily spot this kind because the oil is floating on the surface in the jar. It's a five-minute job to do the mixing. If you store the jar in your refrigerator, you won't have to stir its contents again.

COFFEE AND OTHER DRINKS CONTAINING CAFFEINE

Use Coffee and Other Drinks Containing Caffeine Sparingly. Coffee appears to have many advantages as a stimulant. It is popular, readily available, and low in toxicity. Consequently, millions of us, including myself, use it as a way to raise our energy level. The most logical time to drink coffee is in the morning. It helps us to wake up and get going. Also, there is good evidence suggesting that coffee acts as a cerebral stimulant. Consequently, a cup of coffee can help us concentrate and think through a problem.

The active ingredient in coffee is caffeine, a stimulant found in coffee beans. Other sources of caffeine include tea leaves, cocoa beans, and kola nuts. These sources are used in popular beverages such as tea, cocoa, and cola.

However, there are a few drawbacks to caffeine. Drinking a lot of beverages containing caffeine on an empty stomach can lead to low blood sugar. In turn, low blood sugar is associated with a diminished energy level. Caffeine stimulates the pancreas to secrete additional insulin. This insulin brings the blood sugar down, making you both sluggish and hungry.

If you regularly consume caffeine, you tend to build up a drug tolerance to whatever your regular intake is. Eventually the caffeine doesn't give you a lift. Then you have to take in more in order to get a lift. And then you build up a tolerance to this. Again you have to increase the intake. And so forth. One of my acquaintances was drinking fourteen cups of coffee a day, and it wasn't giving him a lift at all.

A cup of tea contains approximately forty milligrams of caffeine per cup. Strong coffee has about eighty milligrams to a cup. Many people don't recognize that many soft drinks contain caffeine. A typical cola drink will contain between forty and eighty milligrams of caffeine. A cup of cocoa also contains caffeine, but only about ten to twenty milligrams. So don't expect much of a lift from a cup of cocoa. On the contrary, expect an eventual letdown because the principal ingredient in most cocoa mixes is sugar. (Such mixes are now available with artificial sweeteners.)

If, for example, you drink five to eight cups of coffee a day on a regular basis, you can't expect to obtain any particular energy benefit from the practice. You body has almost certainly acquired a tolerance to caffeine. However, let's say that you drink coffee only with breakfast, using it sparingly and irregularly otherwise. Then you can use it from time to time to boost your energy level. It will help to jump-start you when you need it.

DRUGS

Aside From Some Caffeine, Avoid Stimulating Drugs Such as Amphetamines and Cocaine. Amphetamines and cocaine are too powerful to have any practical value in the life of a person who wants to accomplish long-range goals. They do give quick bursts of energy, but then there is a "crash" on the other side. It is much too easy to acquire a psychological dependence upon these drugs. Then the individual doesn't seem to feel either happy or able to accomplish anything without the drug.

ALCOHOL

Avoid Alcohol with Meals That Precede Work. If you face important tasks in the afternoon after lunch, or in the evening after dinner, avoid alcohol with either meal. Like too much food, alcohol lowers central nervous system arousal. You lose alertness and the ability to concentrate when you drink. Consequently, when you want to get things done, don't drink.

The time to drink is when you just want to relax or be sociable and face no particular responsibilities, including driving.

SLEEP

Be Sure You Get an Adequate Amount of Sleep. The average adult needs about seven to eight hours of sleep per night in order to maintain a sense of well-being. However, the need for sleep varies. Some adults need nine and even ten hours of sleep. However, there are many who do well on as little as five or six. If you find yourself waking up early in the morning after a sound sleep, you don't want to necessarily interpret this as a kind of insomnia. Normal sleep patterns have tremendous variability, and it is quite possible that you have had enough sleep. If there are things you want to get done, the morning hours can be optimal ones for some people.

On the other hand, don't kid yourself. If you set the alarm for an early hour and have to force yourself out of bed, it is quite likely that you may induce a gradual sleep deprivation. It is believed that many adults are suffering from a kind of low-grade sleep deprivation. This sort of thing will most definitely undermine your general motivational level and contribute to a tendency to procrastinate.

Afternoon drowsiness is one symptom of sleep deprivation. A simple cure, if you can arrange the time and conditions, is to take a ten- to twenty-minute nap. (Sometimes you can even do this in a chair or a parked car.) My father was in the produce business for a number of years. He got up every morning at 3 A.M., with the exception of Sundays and major holidays, to go to a wholesale market. However, every afternoon he took a twenty-minute nap, stretched out on the seat of his truck. Born and raised in farming country in Italy, he acquired this habit in his youth, and practiced it all of his life. And it served him well.

It is generally unwise to use barbiturates to help you sleep. There is evidence that they inhibit REM sleep (rapid eye movement sleep). A loss of REM sleep appears to have an adverse impact on mood during the day and may be a contributing factor to a lack of interest in life and a general malaise.

CIRCADIAN RHYTHMS

Know Your Own Daily Circadian Pattern. This means be familiar with the times of day when you are naturally at your best, when your arousal is optimal and you function well. The word *circadian* means "something that travels in a circle." The wake-sleep cycle is a principal twenty-four-hour circadian rhythm. Within this overall rhythm you have an individual pattern. For example, some people are "morning people." They can get up at 4 A.M. and be alert and creative. Other people are "evening people" or even "night people." They come alive when others are exhausted. If you know your own pattern, you can "ride" a natural high somewhat in the same way that a surfer rides a wave. As a consequence you can accomplish more with less effort. You work *with* yourself instead of against yourself.

Some of us have two natural highs a day with two natural slumps. Some people have a only a slight variation in their pattern, and can do sustained work at almost any time. Again, it's a good idea to monitor your own pattern and feel confident that you know what it actually is.

The Last Word

The approach taken in this chapter focused on the biological level of behavior. It asserted that although procrastination is usually thought of as a psychological problem, it is certainly true that procrastination is aggravated by a low energy level. In fact, the approach taken in this chapter is somewhat more than biological. To be more accurate, it is what is sometimes called *psychobiological*. A psychobiological approach makes no real distinction between the mind the body. The body affects the mind and the mind affects the body. In fact, at the deepest level they are one. What we call mind is a set of processes including thinking, perception, memory, and decision-making. These processes arise from the activities of the brain and nervous system, which are body. One can hardly expect the mind to function well if the body is not functioning well.

Consequently, in the case of procrastination, it is essential that you keep up your energy level. To repeat the question in the subtitle: How can you want to do anything if you don't have any energy? Well, the answer is obvious. You can't. Or, if you have a low energy level, which is more common than no energy at all, you have to force yourself and drag yourself through your daily activities. And this applies not only to work and tasks, but to recreational activities as well.

A difference in energy level can sometimes be the critical factor that tips the scales in favor of effective action over procrastination.

Assuming that you suffer from neither chronic fatigue syndrome nor from the kind of significant, persistent fatigue that suggests a serious medical problem, take advantage of the practical suggestions made in this chapter. Keep your energy level high.

Key Points to Remember

□— Energy is a vital ingredient in every behavior.

□— Biological drives are sometimes called the *energizers* of behavior.

□— Lack of energy is a common cause of procrastination.

□— There are important distinctions to be made among (1) chronic fatigue syndrome, (2) significant, persistent fatigue, and (3) everyday, garden-variety fatigue.

□— Be sure you have an adequate intake of vitamins and minerals.

□— Be sure that your diet has enough fiber.

□━ Eat light meals.

□━ Have two snacks a day.

□━ Use coffee and other drinks containing caffeine, but sparingly.

□━ Aside from some caffeine, avoid stimulating drugs such as amphetamines and cocaine.

□━ Avoid alcohol with meals that precede work to be done.

□━ Be sure you get an adequate amount of sleep.

□━ Know your own daily circadian pattern.

□━ The approach taken in this chapter is *psychobiological*, making no essential distinction between mind and body.

3 RESISTANCE: DIGGING FOR DEEPER PSYCHOLOGICAL ROOTS

Observed and overheard at a fast-food restaurant:

"Nadine, finish your french fries!"

"No!"

"You've only eaten three or four. They're going to go to waste. I said to finish them!"

"No!"

"But you wanted them. I said you could have some of mine, but you wanted your own."

"Don't care."

"For the last time, finish them."

"No."

The speakers appeared to be a mother and her child. The child, Nadine, was around four years old. The dialogue portrays resistance in action. Toddlers and pre-schoolers often manifest a high level of resistance to the direct commands of their parents. This is usually explained by asserting that at this particular age they have a very great need for autonomy, to declare themselves as individuals. Unfortunately, this need often expresses itself in negative ways.

We all have a "child self" in us. The child self is a carryover from our actual childhood. The child self isn't all bad. It is the source of joy, spontaneity, and to some extent, creativity. However, the child self has its negative aspects. Like an actual child, it can be negative, resistant, and throw temper tantrums. It is this child self, often largely unknown and unexplored, that accounts for much of the resistance associated with procrastination.

Resistance is a psychological force that tends to hinder forward motion. It stops us from acting in a constructive manner. It leads to self-defeat. Resistance is a kind of internal friction, similar to the friction that exists in an internal combustion engine. As we all know, an engine needs oil in order to reduce the level of friction. In a similar way, we need a kind of psychological oil in order to reduce the level of resistance we put in our path.

Sources of Resistance

The child self draws its resistance from many sources. Here are some of the principal ones.

THE NEED FOR AUTONOMY

As already indicated, an actual child may resist a parent because of his or her need for autonomy. The need for autonomy is experienced in both children and adults as a craving for self-direction, as a desire to be in charge of one's own life. When others give us direct orders or get too bossy, we automatically find our need for autonomy frustrated, so we balk, and become negative. We drag our feet. We think, "I don't have to do it."

From the psychological point of view, here's the problem. Your personality also has a parent self and an adult self. The parent self tends to be authoritarian and overly pushy. It is always telling you that you "ought" to do this or that you "should" hurry up or that "you're being a fool" not trying to measure up. The child self's natural response is resistance.

The way out is through the adult self. The adult self is rational, logical, and reality oriented. It can effect a compromise between the child self and the parent self. The suggestions given later in the chapter for overcoming resistance will, to some extent, help to invoke the rational voice of the adult self.

≋≋ ≋≋ ≋≋ ≋≋ ≋≋ ≋≋ ≋≋ ≋≋ ≋≋

FEAR OF FAILURE

Common sense tells us that a principal source of resistance is fear of failure. We often hesitate to take on a difficult task because of anxiety. We imagine the letdown or the disappointment or the embarrassment we will feel if we take a flop. Fletcher M., age twenty-two, has completed most of his courses for a college degree in electronic engineering. His college requires that he take a public speaking course as a graduation requirement. He thinks, "They'll all laugh at me if I goof. I can't speak in public. I never could." Consequently, Fletcher has procrastinated since his first year of college. Instead of getting the public speaking course out of the way early in his academic career, it now looms as a major obstacle to earning his four-year degree.

This semester Fletcher has been sitting next to an attractive young woman named Shannon in his astronomy class. She has been friendly and they have had coffee together several times. He wants to ask her to go out on a date, but keeps procrastinating because he is afraid he'll be turned down. The fantasy that she finds him as attractive as he finds her is more pleasant than the potential reality of rejection. However, his avoidance behavior has a high cost attached to it. He may lose out on the opportunity to have a really rewarding relationship with Shannon.

FEAR OF SUCCESS

It may seem paradoxical to say that fear of success can be a factor in procrastination. It is common sense to assert that fear of failure plays a role in delaying tactics. It is less obvious to say that the opposite of fear of failure, fear of success, also plays a role. Nonetheless, it is true. Fear of success can be a major emotional roadblock.

Megan W., a thirty-three-year-old mother and wife, has completed the first draft of a romance novel. Written

entirely on speculation, she has revised and polished the manuscript several times. It is ready to send to an agent or a publisher. Now she finds herself stuck. She has taken no practical steps in the direction of making an actual submission. Every day she thinks about going to a bookstore and buying a book that lists agents and markets for novels. But that's all she does. She thinks. She doesn't act.

Why?

It's obvious to some degree that she fears failure. Her truck driver husband has been openly critical of her efforts. It upsets her to think that he will have the last laugh if her manuscript is rejected.

However, Megan also fears success. In her imagination success as an author of a novel would open up all sorts of new expectations and additional responsibilities. Would she be a flash in the pan and not be able to write a second novel? Megan has always been a quiet woman who avoided the limelight. Would she have to go on talk shows? Would she have to grant an interview to a local newspaper? She knows that she has a lot of hostility toward her domineering husband. Would she consider leaving him if she became financially independent? It is easy to see how success can be threatening.

INERTIA

Inertia is the initial resistance we all feel to getting started. Everything we do requires taking some first steps. We often find it difficult to take these steps, and this tendency is often one of the biggest barriers to constructive activity.

Imagine a large flywheel. You have to get it turning by sheer muscle power with a crank. It's a dead weight and it's hard to get going. The more it weighs, the more inertia it has. That's resistance at the physical level. You can move the flywheel just a little at first, then more, and then more. Soon you find it spinning rapidly, and it is easy to keep it going with just a little effort.

We are something like that flywheel. It's often hard to get ourselves going. We often find it difficult to be self-starters and "crank" our own behavioral flywheel. However, if we make the effort and discover ways to become more self-starting, we will be rewarded by behavior that flows along with less and less effort.

CHILDHOOD EXPERIENCES

Adverse childhood experiences can be a source of resistance. If something happens in childhood or adolescence that makes you feel inadequate, incompetent, or ineffective, you may readily generalize the experience over to adult life and mistakenly think that the same situation exists in the present.

Kirk N., age thirty-four, hates to write letters. He recently received a letter from an old friend that he hasn't seen in more than a year. He feels that he owes his friend a letter in return, but has been putting off writing for more than three weeks. His resistance to letter writing can be traced back to childhood. Kirk's father, a county judge, used to insist that Kirk write thank-you notes to relatives when he received birthday presents. Kirk remembers writing such notes from the age of seven. He had no resistance to writing them at all, and was more than willing. However, his father would read all of the notes when they were written, criticize them, make corrections in red ink, and insist that Kirk rewrite them. Kirk hated rewriting the notes and soon lost all of his confidence. His youthful spontaneity and honest feelings had been completely undermined. Now when he writes a letter or a memo, the same feelings begin to emerge, and he escapes from them by procrastinating.

You might say that Kirk has an inferiority complex in connection with his ability to write, and you would be correct. The concept of an inferiority complex is important as a factor in procrastination and will be discussed more in chapter 5.

HOSTILITY

Often we procrastinate because of hostility. In most cases this hostility is murky, half-hidden from ourselves. A common situation is one in which one partner harbors resentment toward the other one. Philip G., a successful attorney, provides his second wife with "everything." Renelle has a new car to drive, has a house full of expensive furniture, and belongs to a country club. Renelle is fourteen years younger than Philip and has expressed the desire to go to college and major in oceanography. Philip thinks that this is the silliest thing that he has ever heard and tells her that her full-time job is to be a homemaker— a role that includes being a mother to their children and a hostess to his business associates. Renelle has not really asserted herself, nor made a serious demand that she be supported in her dream of going back to school. Perhaps if she did so Philip would back down.

Philip's main complaint is that Renelle is neglecting little things. She leaves household bills unpaid, and there are often overdue notices. Although she doesn't have daily household help, a person from a service comes in to clean once a week. But that's not enough. As a consequence, the sink is often filled with dirty dishes. Renelle starts dinner late or not at all. She is procrastinating because she is hostile. This kind of procrastination is a part of a passive-aggressive syndrome. The behavior is passive in the sense that she won't openly declare her needs and insist on what she wants. The hostility is bound up in the fact that her procrastination offends and hurts Philip.

When we procrastinate we often hurt or offend someone else. This can be an important factor in resisting constructive action.

THE SIZE OF THE JOB

Sometimes we resist a task because of the sheer size of the job. It just seems too big. We are overwhelmed by its magnitude. Sylvia says, "I put off Christmas shopping every year until the last minute because I have to buy presents for twenty-three people. And I feel that I have to buy just the right present for every person. It's just too much! I feel like I have to climb a mountain every Christmas." Because the job appears to be so large, Sylvia procrastinates and "goes crazy" the last few days before Christmas when the stores are crowded and she "can't find anything."

Olympia G., a city civil engineer, is supposed to finalize a plan and provide a detailed report on a road-widening project. The report has many aspects to it, and Olympia feels she is being asked to do too much in too short a time period. She has let several weeks go by without doing anything about the report.

Overcoming Resistance

Earlier in this chapter I compared resistance to the friction produced when a motor is in motion. And I also noted that we need a kind of psychological oil in order to reduce the level of resistance we experience when we try to act. The suggestions that follow are this "oil." They recognize the nature of resistance, and can readily be used to overcome its drag on action. Of course, oil in a can doesn't do a motor any good. The can has to be opened and the oil poured into the crankcase. Similarly, you have to act on these suggestions in order for them to do you any good.

WHY

Ask Yourself Why You Are Resisting. Don't take a superficial approach to problem procrastination. Dig for deeper psychological roots. Strive to understand yourself and to develop insight into *why* you resist effective action. It is best to do this *in writing.* Writing things out helps to focus your attention and clarify a problem. Ask yourself the following questions:

1. Am I resisting and procrastinating because of a need for autonomy?

2. Am I resisting constructive action because of a fear of failure?

3. Am I resisting working toward my goals because of a fear of success?

4. Am I allowing childhood experiences to be a source of resistance and procrastination?

5. Am I resisting and procrastinating as a way of expressing hostility toward someone else?

Write out short answers to the questions with examples from your own life. When you bring hidden feelings out of the darkness of their psychological basement into

the light of day, they often can be seen to be flimsy fantasies with little real substance. They are like ghosts that fly away when you say, "Boo!"

Understanding why you procrastinate is important. But it is not sufficient. In order to actually overcome procrastination you need some skills and techniques. These are presented in the suggestions that follow. They go beyond the *why* and focus on the *how*.

RESOLUTIONS

Don't Make "Good" Resolutions. What? Don't make good resolutions? What could be more foolish advice? Everyone "knows" that the way to get things done is to make a resolution. People make good resolutions on New Year's Eve. And most of these resolutions are broken in a few days. One problem with good resolutions is their very goodness. The word *good* implies a value judgment. It automatically suggests an *ought* or a *should*. It is a form of internal moralizing. It arises from your parent self, and your child self resents it. Consequently, the net effect of a good resolution usually does not activate your positive will, but your *counterwill*. The counterwill is a negative tendency in you that says, "I don't *have* to do it." Think back to Nadine who said, "No!" when her mother told her to finish her french fries.

Don't put yourself into a straitjacket with a good resolution. You will only want to tear it off. Instead, think in terms of effective behavior, of getting in touch with your reality-oriented adult self. Stay focused on the here and the now and on what you can actually *do* in the present to overcome procrastination. The suggestions that follow will help you do this.

THE TISSUE-PAPER BARRIER

Poke Your Finger Through the Tissue-Paper Barrier. Edward M. is an architect, the owner of his own small firm. He specializes in designing custom homes for wealthy people. They want creative designs, but they also want functional homes. Often he is presented with requests that seem absurd. Frequently he has to design homes for "impossible" lots with strange shapes and odd slopes. He says, "For years I had a problem with procrastination. I had a hard time sitting down to my drawing board and making sketches because I thought that my clients were unreasonable. They made me angry with some of their silly requests. I used to think that their money made them spoiled. I realize now that I was threatened more than angry. I didn't think I could come through. For some reason I visualized a huge block of granite in my way, and I had to move it aside before I could get down to real work. Then one day, don't ask me why, a different image came to my mind. I saw a needlework hoop with tissue paper snapped into place instead of cloth. And I thought to myself, 'That's it! My hesitance is just a tissue-paper barrier. It's not a block of granite. And I'm just putting the barrier in my own way.' So I decided all that I have to do is to poke a finger through the tissue-paper barrier, and I'll be able to get to work. Now whenever I find myself putting off getting down to brass tacks on a new project, I visualize a hoop with tissue paper. Then in my mind's eye I see my finger poking through it, and then I simply go to my desk and make a start. It really helps."

Use Edward's technique as one way to overcome initial resistance. The mind is a powerful image maker. Negative images can act as major barriers to behavior. And positive images can facilitate effective behavior.

THE SEAT OF THE CHAIR

Apply the Seat of the Pants to the Seat of the Chair. Twyla R. is a freelance medical transcriber. She has several physician accounts. She brings home audio tapes dictated by the physician, and converts them into written case records. She works at a word processor, and the work is demanding and detailed. It requires an accurate knowledge of medical terms. The work is well paid and is in some ways an ideal career choice because she makes her own hours and can also function as a wife and mother of two children. Unfortunately, she has to start and stop many times a day, and she often experiences resistance. It is all too easy to procrastinate, and at one time she was falling far behind in her work.

Twyla says, "One afternoon I was doing everything but getting down to making transcriptions. I baked a cake. I began to reread Charlotte Brontë's *Jane Eyre*. I knew I was procrastinating, and I felt helpless. Then I remembered reading an article in a magazine for creative writers that writing was mainly 90 percent perspiration and 10 percent inspiration. The author of the article went on to say that writing is mainly applying the seat of the pants to the seat of the chair. 'That's it!' I thought. Medical transcription is hardly creative writing. But the basic trick is the same: Apply the seat of the pants to the seat of the chair. I immediately got up and did just that. I sat down in the chair in front of my word processor. Well, then, now what else could I do but to turn it on? So I did. Then what else could I do but get to work? And I did. Now whenever I want to get started I just say to myself, 'Apply the seat of the pants to the seat of the chair.' And it works."

Think about how many activities and tasks require sitting down at a word processor or a desk. Here's a short list: paying bills, studying, writing a report, getting taxes ready, sending out holiday cards, and composing thank-you notes. Whenever you find yourself using delaying tactics in order to avoid such tasks, think, "Apply the seat of the pants to the seat of the chair."

A HALF-BAKED START

Make a Half-Baked Start. Remember that any start is better than no start. You don't have to make a good start, a smart start, or even a start in the right direction. All you have to do is to make a start. The quality of what you do is not at first important. Depending on the task or project, you can often go back to the beginning and modify what you have done. People often say when facing a formidable task, "I don't know where to start." This remark becomes an excuse for inaction. The right way to deal with the task is to think, "I'll start anywhere. It doesn't make any difference where I start."

Wilma D. had a closet that was filled with all kinds of things she wanted to discard: old clothes, shoes, wrapping paper, patterns, magazines, and much more. For three years she thought, "I don't know where to start." She was telling her sister this one day, and her sister asked, "Why not just start anywhere?" The question stuck. And Wilma thought, "Why not? Why not just start anywhere?" The next day she opened the closet and instead of feeling overwhelmed decided she would go through the shoes and sort out the ones she wanted to keep and the ones she wanted to get rid of. The choice of shoes was completely arbitrary. Maybe it wasn't the best place to start, but it was a start.

Making a half-baked start is good advice whenever you have any writing to do. Just start writing and don't worry too much about the quality. You can always throw out the first paragraph or two. The idea is to get going, to start some kind of flow.

Remember the wisdom of the Chinese sage Lao-tzu who said, "The journey of a thousand miles begins with a single step." Take the first small step. Make almost any kind of a beginning, and you will find that the journey has begun.

CHALLENGING TASKS

Don't Tell Yourself a Task Is Difficult, Tell Yourself It Is Challenging. There is a world of difference between the words *difficult* and *challenging.* If you think of a task as difficult, you see it as a formidable obstacle, as a barrier to accomplishment, and as a source of frustration. On the other hand, if you think of a task as challenging, you see it as an opportunity to show your ability, as a source of potential pride in accomplishment, as an opportunity to grow as a person. There is something to be learned from all chores, assignments, and projects. Think of no task as difficult. <u>Always mentally substitute the word *challenging* in place of *difficult*.</u>

Key Points to Remember

□— Resistance is a psychological force that tends to hinder forward motion.

□— Important sources of resistance include (1) the need for autonomy, (2) a fear of failure, (3) a fear of success, (4) <u>inertia</u>, (5) adverse childhood experiences, (6) hostility, and (7) the large size of a job.

□— <u>Ask yourself why you are resisting.</u>

□— Don't make "good" resolutions.

□— Poke your finger through the tissue-paper barrier. Apply the seat of the pants to the seat of the chair.

□— Make a half-baked start.

□— Don't tell yourself that a task is difficult; tell yourself that it is challenging.

4 STOP KIDDING YOURSELF: TIME TO FACE REALITY

Byron L. has just put some gas in his car on his way home from work. He looks at the tires and they seem to be low. He thinks about the water and the oil, realizing he hasn't checked the fluid levels recently. He thinks, "I'm too tired to put air in the tires and to look under the hood right now. I'll do it tomorrow morning, bright and early, on my way to work." He hops in the car and heads home.

The question is: Is he *really* too tired? Or is he just using the *idea* of being tired as a feeble excuse to avoid a responsibility? As indicated in chapter 2, there often *is* such a thing as genuine fatigue, and it can be a factor in procrastination. However, it is also quite possible that imaginary fatigue can be produced to allow oneself to get away with an unnecessary delay or otherwise irresponsible behavior. When this happens, the individual is kidding himself or herself.

We are great at kidding ourselves.

Unfortunately, this tendency, while momentarily comforting, can keep us from effective behavior. It can have long-run adverse consequences in the real world.

Consequently, whenever you can, it is a good idea to stop kidding yourself.

Ego Defense Mechanisms

The words *kidding yourself* provide an informal designation for a process associated with the *ego defense mechanisms*. The concept of ego defense mechanisms was first clearly articulated in psychology by Freud. His daughter, Anna, elaborated on their importance in everyday affairs. An ego defense mechanism is an automatic reaction. Its purpose is to protect the ego against the harsher aspects of reality. The ego is the "I" of the personality, the conscious center of the human self. The ego often perceives itself as weak, as fragile, as needing protection. Consequently, it produces barriers between itself and reality.

Think of a medieval knight in armor. He needs protection against arrows, swords, lances, and clubs. However, there is a problem. If he wears too much armor, his movements become cumbersome. He is awkward. He can't fight effectively. On the other hand, if he wears no armor at all, he is vulnerable. A single arrow might kill him. What is the solution? Many knights rode into battle wearing light armor. This gave them some protection and at the same time they were effective warriors.

This is a good way to think about ego defense mechanisms. Each one is a kind of armor. If you use all of them most of the time you will be as restrained and as ineffective as a medieval knight wearing heavy armor. Your ego will be protected. You will be psychologically safe. Nothing can touch you. No one can reach you. But you won't accomplish much.

The aim of this chapter is not to get you to give up your ego defense mechanisms. That would be as absurd as telling a knight to go into battle naked. You need some protection. The human personality is designed in such a way that its defense mechanisms are essential to its functioning.

However, you don't want to abuse your defense mechanisms. You don't want to rely on them when you don't really need to. You want to be able to set them aside whenever they restrict your forward motion in life. Abusing them can result in prolonged delays between an opportunity and the effective behavior that should arise from it.

Avoiding Defense Mechanisms

The balance of this chapter will define the principal defense mechanisms and how they work. You will learn how they often keep you going either nowhere or in circles. In each case, the practical suggestion begins with the word *avoid*. It is a central assumption of this chapter that it is possible to learn to avoid excessive reliance on the ego defense mechanisms. They are usually presented as automatic and involuntary, as arising from the unconscious domain. If you take this viewpoint, and this viewpoint alone, you will be the helpless victim of your own defense mechanisms. However, it is also true that you have a "creative self." This was an idea proposed by Alfred Adler, one of the early founders of psychoanalysis. The creative self is the self in you that can rise above circumstances, that can see into the future, that can wrestle with the ego defense mechanisms and put them in their proper place. Use your creative self to cope with your own self-defeating tendencies.

DENIAL OF REALITY

Avoid the Use of Denial of Reality. Denial of reality takes place when an individual is presented with information and then rejects the obvious meaning of the information. It is a primitive mechanism and a favorite choice of the preschooler. Four-year-old Nicole was told that there was to be a family picnic this Sunday. Sunday turns out to be a rainy day. Sadly, her mother imparts the bad news. "It's raining, sweetheart. And we won't be able to go on the picnic after all."

Nicole appears glum for a moment. Then she looks out the window. Her face brightens. "It's going to stop pretty soon." There is no rational basis for Nicole's assertion. The sun isn't peeking through the clouds. The rain is not slowing down. The assertion arises totally from her *wish*, the wish that the rain would stop so the family can go on the picnic.

Garfield R. is driving on the freeway toward his home in the suburbs. He glances at his gas gauge and it displays "empty." He pictures the familiar station near home where he likes to stop. He doesn't want to pull off of the freeway. He thinks, "I'll wait. I've probably got some extra gas in the tank. They build a margin of error into these things." So he keeps cruising merrily along in a fool's paradise. He isn't so happy a little later when he is stranded several miles between off-ramps, his car out of gas. He used denial of reality. He allowed his wishful thinking to override his realistic thinking, and he paid the price.

Stephanie H. has a master of arts degree and teaches English composition part time at a local community college. She teaches two classes, and is also a wife and a mother. She loves the work and hopes someday to receive a contract and a full-time job. The head of the department calls her in and tells her that she always gets her grades in after the school deadline. This has happened two semesters in a row. Sometimes she has been as much as two to three weeks late. Stephanie is told that unless she gets her grades in on time this semester, she will be let go and not rehired.

Stephanie tells the department head that she will get the grades in promptly. However, when the semester ends several weeks later, she has more important things to do than to grade final compositions and make a tally of semester scores. Again, she delays. The department head's warning nags at her. However, Stephanie thinks, "He didn't mean it." And there it is. In that simple four-word sentence there is a complete denial of reality. When Stephanie is not given a job offer for the fall semester, she is much put out and tells her husband that she has been treated very unfairly.

When other people or circumstances hand you free information on a plate, don't reject it because it is unpalatable. You have to take it in. You have to assimilate it and accommodate it. Granted, this can often be very difficult to do.

The following story shows how the mind can bend facts to maintain a denial of reality. A man makes an appointment to see a clinical psychologist. When he enters the office, the psychologist invites him to sit down and asks, "What is your problem?"

The man says, "I'm dead."

"You're dead?"

"Yes."

"Do dead men bleed?"

"Of course not."

"Give me your finger."

The psychologist pricks it with a pin and squeezes out a drop of blood.

"Now what do you say?"

The man stares at the finger for a moment. Then he looks at the psychologist and says, "You know. You're right. Dead men do bleed."

Don't be like this man. Accommodate facts. Allow them to change your outlook and in turn change your behavior. You can't be effective in the real world by denying its very reality.

RATIONALIZATION

Avoid the Use of Rationalization. *Rationalization* occurs when one gives oneself a superficially plausible reason for an ineffective, irresponsible, or otherwise nonfunctional action. The reason is seemingly "rational" in nature. It looks good. It appears to be logical. But it is, in fact, a sham. It is falsely presented by the mind to itself in order to soothe the ego.

The example of Byron L. presented in the opening paragraph of this chapter provided an instance of rationalization. Let's say that he wasn't really too tired to inflate his tires. If so, he used fatigue as a seemingly logical reason to avoid responsible behavior.

Alice G. is a secretary in the science department of a small college. She has two part-time student assistants. She is frequently behind in her work, missing important deadlines. Instructors complain that tests are not ready on schedule. From the point of view of others, her behavior borders on the unacceptable. From Alice's own point of view, she rationalizes, "They give me too much too do. What do they think I am, a mule? No one could keep up with this workload." The fact is that with her two assistants, and the general nature of the job, she is not having too much imposed on her. She procrastinates. There are things she would rather do than her work. She is alone in the office for ten- and twenty-minute periods several times a day. Although she is entitled to, and takes, regular breaks, she also thinks of these periods of solitude as opportunities to take a break. She calls a friend on the phone, reads a magazine, has a snack and a cup of coffee, and fritters away her time. She has been threatened with dismissal. Unless she faces facts and stops rationalizing, she is in danger of losing her job.

Rationalization is a way of excusing yourself just a little too readily for a personal deficit. Try to catch yourself in the act of rationalizing, and it will help you to avoid doing it.

REGRESSION

Avoid the Use of Regression. Many, perhaps most, children know the art of procrastination well. It is often very difficult to get them to engage in responsible behavior. They frequently have to be nagged to clean up a room, to do a few chores, to get their homework done, to get dressed to go visiting, and so forth. Why? If asked for a reason, they feel the very question is unreasonable. They are not self-analytical. All they know is that they don't want to do it right now. They'll do it later when they "feel" like it. If you are the parent of a child who procrastinates too much, you might want to obtain a copy of a book called _Morgan and Me_ by Stephen Cosgrove. It tells the story of an unnamed Little Princess who lives in the Land of Later. She eventually rescues a trapped unicorn named Morgan and learns an important lesson about the importance of not procrastinating.

In the case of adults, *regression* is a defense mechanism in which the ego retreats in the direction of behavior that is more suitable to a child than to an adult. Informally, we often say that another person is being "childish."

There is a Little Prince or a Little Princess in all of us who thinks that he or she is just a bit above having to wash the dishes now or mow the lawn now or cook dinner now or start dressing for an appointment now, and so forth. We all like to live in the Land of Later. But, unfortunately, living in the Land of Later has eventual costs that may not be worth any pleasures associated with delay. When you want to live in the Land of Later, you are allowing your child self to take over. You are regressing.

Observe your own behavior. Ask yourself, "Am I regressing? And I living in the Land of Later?" If the answer to either question is yes, it will draw you up short and allow you to redirect your energies in a more responsible direction.

PROJECTION

Avoid the Use of Projection. Projection takes place when we perceive either an external factor or another person as the principal source causing us to fail to live up to our own expectations. It is *it* or *him* or *her* that is causing us to slow down or avoid or not get things done. The concept of projection can readily be associated with the Rorschach test, a test used to evaluate personality. The subject is shown inkblots. They are ambiguous stimuli, in and of themselves just formless blobs, nothing at all. Asked to be imaginative, persons "see" all sorts of things in the inkblots ranging from wild animals to puppets dancing on strings. What a subject sees is, of course, not something seen at all, but a perception. The perception is constructed by the unconscious level of the mind, and it is "projected," like a slide projector, onto the inkblot. The subject's perceptions, or projections, reveal unconscious motives and emotional conflicts.

Something like the inkblot process takes place in daily life. Situations are often poorly defined. Others are often manipulative or deceptive, consequently presenting themselves in an ambiguous manner. We will almost certainly "see" something in both the situations or the people we deal with, but frequently this seen something is unreal and just our own projection.

As a consequence of our tendency to project, we often play the Blaming Game. The Blaming Game reassigns the locus of control for our behavior from the self to the external world.

Hayley R. is twenty pounds overweight. She says to her sister, "I want to start a diet. But I can't. Harry expects home-cooked meals at least five nights a week. And he loves my apple pies. When I'm cooking like this for him, there's just no way I can lose weight." Her statements indicate that she is using projection as a delaying tactic. She blames being a traditional homemaker and her husband Harry for her weight problem. A cold look at her situation suggests that home-cooked meals can be low in both fat and calories and that Harry should lose some weight too. By giving up projection, Hayley might see that her situation is a *golden opportunity* to eat right and lose weight. Interestingly, people who work at a daily outside job often blame the fact that they eat on the run, have to buy fast foods, and can't plan meals, for excessive pounds.

David H., a mechanical engineer, is in line for an important promotion. His employer, however, requires first that Harry take a class in advanced aspects of calculus at a local college. David says, "I can't get the promotion because I can't take the class. It's given only at night and it's at a bad time for me, 7 to 10 P.M. on Thursday night. If I take a class like that, I'll be shot the next day. And the boss shouldn't ask me to take the class anyway. I know enough calculus to do the job." As long as David thinks like this, he will not get promoted. He is refusing to play ball in accordance with his employer's rules, and he is projecting the blame for his failure on the hour of the class and his employer's "unreasonable" request.

If you detect a certain overlap between rationalization and projection, or among the defense mechanisms, this is natural. After all, they all belong to the same general class. Although each one is fairly well defined, the borders between them do blur to some extent.

Examine a delay in behavior in terms of projection. Ask yourself, "Am I blaming something or someone else for my avoidance tendencies? Am I incorrectly placing the locus of control in the external world?"

DISPLACEMENT OF AGGRESSION

Avoid the Use of Displacement of Aggression. Let's say that you feel you are entitled to a raise. It is long overdue in your opinion, and your employer has made no gesture to increase your salary. You are determined to discuss matters with your employer and to ask for a raise. However, you keep procrastinating. You resist the encounter. You imagine that it can turn unpleasant. You fear its adverse consequences. So you are feeling hostile. Frustration begets aggression, and you want to take out your hostility on someone, anyone.

So you pick a little fight with your partner. Perhaps you find fault with the way the other person does things around the house. Or maybe you criticize one of your children severely for a minor infraction. In both of these examples you are displacing your aggression on a target that is safer than your employer. *Displacement of aggression* occurs when aggressive behavior is shifted from its original source to a substitute one. It is also called *scapegoating*. It's unfair to the scapegoats. They are innocent victims. And it keeps you procrastinating by draining off the aggressive energy that should be constructively directed to the source of frustration.

If you find yourself being a little too mean to a partner or to your children, ask yourself if you are displacing aggression. Maybe you are aiming your hostile arrows at the wrong target. Make an effort to aim in the right direction.

REACTION FORMATION

Avoid the Use of Reaction Formation. Reaction formation is a defense mechanism in which a wish or feeling repressed to the unconscious level converts itself into its own opposite at a conscious level. The blocked psychological element does a kind of flip-flop and turns itself upside down. Veronica T. has been married for several years. She has a problem with her mother-in-law, Wanda. Wanda drops in unannounced several times a week, tells her how to cook, informs her that her son doesn't really like what she's fixing for dinner, gives Veronica unsolicited advice on how to raise her toddler son, and so forth. When her mother-in-law shows up, Veronica feels like screaming. She has discussed the problem with her husband, James. He says, "Talk things over with her. Tell her how you feel. Don't put her down, but negotiate something. Tell her you need more space."

"That sounds easy," Veronica says.

"What else can you do? You can't just go on enduring this. Do you want me to talk to her? I will."

"No. It's my problem. Let me deal with it."

But Veronica keeps putting off any realistic solution. Her behavior is, in fact, quite the opposite of what it should be. She is supersweet to her mother-in-law. When Wanda appears, she is always invited in with a warm greeting, offered coffee, and made to feel at home. When Wanda makes a suggestion, Veronica receives it with a smile, often saying something like, "What a good idea!" Veronica's conscious sweetness is a way of holding back her hidden hostility. It is a reaction formation.

A reaction formation is the wrong strategy to use in this case because it perpetuates the problem. Wanda is being rewarded for her inappropriate behavior. Veronica is procrastinating in one of the worst ways possible. Instead of dealing with the problem in the present, she is deferring it to some vague future. And the problem is getting worse.

If you find yourself being overly sweet to someone else, ask yourself if your pleasant behavior is a mask over hostility. Examine your real feelings. Ask yourself if reaction formation is being used as an ineffective delaying tactic.

NARCISSISM

Avoid the Use of Narcissism. Perhaps you are familiar with the Greek myth of Narcissus. He fell in love with his own image in a pool of water and wasted away as he yearned to make an impossible connection with it. *Narcissism* is a defense mechanism characterized by excessive preoccupation with the self. A person with strong narcissistic tendencies finds it difficult to feel real love for others. Jeffrey G. is married and has an eight-year-old son, Mitchell. Jeffrey is a very handsome tall man with broad shoulders and a narrow waist. He acts as if he's God's gift to women. He has several pieces of exercise equipment in his home and spends an inordinate amount of time working out on them. He would like to have a better relationship with his son. Somehow he doesn't know how to relate. He can't hug Mitchell or laugh with him. He knows that the only way to improve his relationship is to spend time with him, to get to know Mitchell as a person. But Jeffrey's preoccupation with self is excessive. Recently Mitchell interrupted his father while he was in the middle of one of his exercise routines. Mitchell wanted to know if his father could play a game with him. Jeffrey growled at Mitchell, "Not now, son. Can't you see this is a bad time? Maybe later." But later never came. One of the psychological functions of narcissism in Jeffrey's life is to buy him time away from others, time that might be spent constructively working toward emotional closeness. But this is something he wants to avoid.

There are milder ways to use narcissism in daily living. Let's say that you have a reputation of being a slowpoke. When the rest of the family is ready to go out the door for a special occasion, you are still combing your hair for the second time, changing your clothes for the third time, or doing something similar to keep from actually leaving the house. You are using a narcissistic tendency in yourself—an excessive preoccupation with your appearance—as a way of stalling. Perhaps you have mixed

feelings about the group of people you will be seeing. Maybe you imagine that they will be critical of your appearance. You are resisting going at all to some extent, and you overly focus on your self-image as a procrastination device.

Look at your own behavior. Ask yourself if you are overly absorbed in yourself. Does such self-absorption cause you to put off more important things? Care about yourself, yes. But avoid caring to the point of preoccupation.

IDENTIFICATION

Avoid Identifying with the Wrong Person. There is someone you admire. You would like to have his or her traits or attributes. This is one of the reasons we read fiction and go to movies. We enjoy identifying with the heroes and heroines in stories, particularly protagonists who succeed in their endeavors. *Identification* takes place when you unconsciously link your ego with the ego of another, drawing strength or solace from the association. It can be a functional defense mechanism, working to strengthen your sense of worth. On the other hand, it can be a dysfunctional mechanism if you identify with the wrong person.

Let's say that a person you admire for certain traits also has the trait of procrastination. You may pick up some of the positive traits, such as courage or creativity. But the negative trait of procrastination will also rub off on you. So be careful whom you identify with. Pick your role models carefully. If you have a strong tendency to procrastinate, be very careful that you avoid identifying with others who also procrastinate.

FANTASY

Don't Use Fantasy as a Way to Evade Responsibility. All of us know what it is to daydream, to build castles in the air. There is nothing intrinsically wrong with this activity. On the contrary, daydreaming can be a source of inspiration. It can help you to visualize your goals. Sometimes in your mind's eye you can see the path leading toward the life you really want to lead and the person you really want to become.

However, fantasy can also be a defense mechanism. In this situation fantasy is used to evade responsibility. Let's say that your fantasies tend to be ones in which your role is passive. You are rewarded just for existing. You win the lottery. A rich relative leaves you a fortune. A beautiful or a handsome stranger approaches you and says that you

are very attractive. You are given an honorary Ph.D. A physician discovers a cure for obesity that makes you slim. In all of these kinds of fantasies you do not have to take an active role; you are not the agent of your own change. Note that your role is to wait. As the psychiatrist Eric Berne, author of *Games People Play*, used to say, "This is waiting for Santa Claus." We assert that as adults we don't believe in Santa Claus. But it appears, unconsciously at least, that many of us engage in a kind of wishful thinking that feeds procrastination.

Ask yourself if you overindulge in passive fantasies. If you do, make an attempt to short circuit them as they start to involuntarily present themselves in your mind's eye. Instead, make an effort to actively substitute a fantasy in which you see yourself *doing something* to reach a goal.

REPRESSION

Reflect on the Nature of Repression. *Repression* is a defense mechanism in which a previously conscious idea or motive is banished to the unconscious level of the personality. The mental action is involuntary. The ideas or motives banished are those that are unacceptable to the conscious self, that do violence to one's values and moral standards. Repression is the master defense mechanism that underlies all of the defense mechanisms. I have saved it for last because it does not at first appear to be accessible to the conscious mind and to rational analysis. You will note that the above suggestion does not say to "avoid" repression, but to "reflect" on it.

It is important to realize that the process of repression takes place in all of us, that to some extent we have forbidden wishes and traits we find unacceptable. One of the ways to unravel the negative effects of repression on your life is by avoiding the other defense mechanisms, the ones that have already been identified. You do have a certain amount of conscious access to these. You can learn to catch yourself in the act. You don't have to be their victim. These constructive actions on your part will undercut repression in general, and you will be in better touch with yourself.

THE TENNIS-BALL EGO

Picture Your Ego as a Tennis Ball. Here is an excerpt from the journal of Roberta F., a forty-four-year-old wife, mother, and computer software engineer:

I used to think of my ego as a fragile Christmas tree ornament. It had to be very carefully protected against the slings and arrows of outrageous fortune. Like an ornament, if dropped it would break. I used to think about myself that way. "This will shatter me." "I'll go to pieces if he finds out." Consequently, I was touchy and defensive—always on guard.

Then one day I happened to watch some people playing tennis. I saw the ball getting batted all over the place without much apparent damage. I thought, "Why can't my ego be like that ball? Why does it have to be fragile, like an ornament?" Then I thought, "Why indeed? I'm just choosing images. For some reason I've chosen the image of the ornament. I can make a conscious switch and choose the image of the ball." I thought about the attributes of a tennis ball. It is tough and resilient. It bounces back. "That's me," I thought. "I always bounce back. I'm tougher than I think I am."

I decided to consciously picture a tennis-ball ego. And it has helped me to distance myself from the self-defeating defense mechanisms that keep me from being effective.

Like Roberta, you can make a conscious choice. Try picturing your ego as a tennis ball, and decide that you have the adaptability to accept reality in a constructive way. It will help you to take effective action and stop procrastinating.

The Last Word

You don't have to be the victim of your own ego defense mechanisms. You don't have to be stuck in psychological mud because you keep kidding yourself. Remember the concept of the creative self. You have intelligence and imagination. You can rise above mental mechanisms and control your own behavior. The ego defense mechanisms are like weights. They drag you down. They slow you down. They are excess baggage. They *do* provide a kind of sugar coating over the pill or reality. But this sugar coating is a bad bargain because it tends to stop you from actually doing what you need to do.

Key Points to Remember

□— An ego defense mechanism is an automatic reaction. Its purpose is to protect the ego against the harsher aspects of reality.

□— The "creative self" is the self in you that can rise above circumstances, that can see into the future, that can wrestle with the ego defense mechanisms and put them in their proper place.

□— Avoid the use of denial of reality.

□— Avoid the use of rationalization.

□— Avoid the use of regression.

□— Avoid the use of projection.

□— Avoid the use of displacement of aggression.

□— Avoid the use of reaction formation.

□— Avoid the use of narcissism.

□— Avoid identifying with the wrong person.

□— Don't use fantasy as a way to evade responsibility.

□— Reflect on the nature of repression.

□— Picture your ego as a tennis ball.

□— Using the creative self, you can rise above defense mechanisms and control your own behavior.

5 SUBDUING AN INFERIORITY COMPLEX: TURNING A MINUS INTO A PLUS

I recall seeing a cartoon a few years ago that depicted a patient reclining on a couch. The therapist was saying, "I have just figured out your problem, Mr. Jones. You don't have an inferiority complex. You *are* inferior."

The humor, of course, is at the cost of people who suffer from self doubt. But let's stand the joke on its head. The truth of the matter is that most people who are troubled by feelings of inadequacy magnify their defects and minimize their good points. And they *are not* inferior; they just think they are.

What is an inferiority complex?

How does an inferiority complex contribute to procrastination?

How can you subdue an inferiority complex?

These questions will be answered in this chapter.

The Will to Power

Alfred Adler, one of the pioneers of psychotherapy, was the psychologist who introduced the concept of the inferiority complex. He said that all human beings have an inborn will to power. He derived this idea from the writings of the philosopher Friedrich Nietzsche. The will to power, as Adler understood it, is a constructive force. It is a desire to grow, to learn, to become all that you can become. Most children *want* to learn to ride a bicycle, dress themselves, and read. Adults *want* to become competent, effective, and reach their goals.

Unfortunately, the will to power is often blocked. Parents can be much less nurturing than they ought to be. Some parents discount their children's accomplishments. Still others are abusive. Siblings may outdistance you in motor skills or academic achievements. Peers can be cruel and call you nicknames because of a flaw in your appearance such as being overweight or taller than average. Nicknames such as "Fatso" and "Beanpole" contribute to a negative self-image.

As a consequence of the frustration of the will to power, an inferiority complex is born. The very existence of an inferiority complex, particularly in childhood and adolescence, contributes to its malignant growth. Thirteen-year-old Dru thinks that she is not pretty. Consequently, she resists all efforts on her mother's part to dress her in "cute" dresses, to curl her hair, and to improve her appearance in general. She thinks that such efforts are acts of futility, and that her peers will laugh at her for her pathetic efforts. Fourteen-year-old Julian has had the nickname of "Fatso" ever since the fifth grade. Because he is fat he feels lonely. He often eats out of self-pity. This makes him fatter and lonelier.

How can an inferiority complex play a role in procrastination?

Let's say that Julian is now a twenty-four-year-old man. He is a college graduate and an auto insurance underwriter. One of the coworkers in the office is Rowena, who works in customer service. Julian finds Rowena very attractive and would like to ask her out on a date. He has a silent crush on Rowena. He has reached an age when marriage is a possibility. He fantasizes that a date might lead to love, marriage, and a family. On the realistic level, he has a good relationship with Rowena. The two of them kid around a lot, sometimes go on coffee break together, but Julian is afraid that she would prefer that they remain "just friends."

Julian is still a little overweight, but not much—maybe ten or fifteen pounds. However, he still has an "I'm too fat" inferiority complex. Objectively, he is actually reasonably good looking. He is well educated. He's a desirable male. But he doesn't *feel* good looking or desirable. At a subconscious level, he still perceives himself as a lonely fat child. Because of his inferiority complex he lets the weeks turn into months. He doesn't ask Rowena for a date. He stands helplessly by as another man dates her and eventually marries her. Julian feels like a victim.

It is time to define an inferiority complex. An inferiority complex is a set of interrelated negative ideas about some aspect of the self. It is specific. For example, it is possible to have an inferiority complex concerning your:

> stature
>
> <u>weight</u>
>
> mathematical ability
>
> verbal ability
>
> social poise
>
> <u>facial features</u>
>
> age
>
> intelligence
>
> creativity

And the list could be extended. Note that it is possible to have more than one inferiority complex. You can think that you are both bad at math and socially inept. Although an inferiority complex is specific, its poison spreads throughout your personality.

This brings us to the relationship between an inferiority complex and self-esteem. <u>An inferiority complex contributes to low self-esteem. Self-esteem is a kind of rating. It is a subjective measure of your perceived worth</u>. If your self-esteem falls too low, you feel worthless. In contrast, if you have high self-esteem, you tend to be sustained by a sense of personal worth.

Overcoming an inferiority complex will help you improve your self-esteem. And it will help you stop procrastinating in important areas of your life.

Subduing an Inferiority Complex

Fortunately, your personality has a natural tendency that works against inferiority complexes. You need to discover this natural tendency and make it work more effectively for you. This tendency is a psychological process called *compensation*. Compensation is an ego defense mechanism. However, unlike the ones discussed in the prior chapter, compensation has a life-enhancing effect. Its principal purpose is to help you overcome an inferiority complex. Adler called compensation the marvelous ability of the personality to turn a psychological minus into a plus.

Here is an actual example. A boy was thought to be dull or even mentally retarded by his teachers. He was poor and as a child sold candy on a train to make a living. He was hard of hearing. He had no powerful connections in the business world as a young adult. People laughed at his odd ideas. It sounds like this individual should have had a load of inferiority complexes. And he did. But he overcame them by the process of compensation. He worked harder than others to prove his worth. He decided to believe in himself no matter what others thought. He developed the trait of persistence. Little by little he overcame all of the barriers to success. He married and became wealthy and famous. He had more patents to his name than any other inventor in U.S. history, more than a thousand. His name? Thomas Alva Edison.

You and I probably don't have half as much to overcome as Edison. If he could accomplish his dreams and goals, so can you. Below you will find a number of practical suggestions that will help you subdue an inferiority complex.

MISTAKES

Don't Be Afraid to Make Mistakes. Think about toddlers learning to walk. They make nothing but mistakes at first. They aren't coordinated. They don't have their balance. They fall. But they pick themselves up and keep trying and eventually succeed. An inferiority complex may make you think that you have to do everything smoothly and perfectly the first time. In your imagination this is what other people do. You see someone accomplished in some way who has something you lack in terms of social poise or appearance, and you incorrectly imagine that all such people are naturals, that their abilities come naturally to them. You cannot see the history of trial and error behind their present behavior. Try to be aware that a lot of learning goes into almost all accomplished performance. Think to yourself, "Trial and error is a basic process in learning." And perhaps you will be more willing to make mistakes.

Let's go back to Edison. It is well known that he tried hundreds of substances on an almost random hit-or-miss basis before he found the right filament for the electric lightbulb. All of his trials were errors except for one. But it only took one success. And it led to the first practical lightbulb. Edison wasn't afraid to make mistakes, and neither should you be.

BIOGRAPHIES

Become Familiar With the Biographies of Effective People. There are many ways to do this. Every bookstore and library has a large section devoted to biographies. Many motion pictures, available on videotape, dramatize the lives of famous people. Perhaps one of your cable channels carries the series called *Biography*.

You will learn that effective people almost always have had one or several inferiority complexes in their past. Or, to put it more accurately, they have found ways to subdue their inferiority complexes. An inferiority complex has a way of hanging around and lurking in the shadows no matter how much you accomplish. But you can *subdue* it. You can keep it in the shadows through the mechanism of compensation. In fact, when you become adept at doing this, compensation for an inferiority complex becomes a motivating factor. This, again, is what is meant by turning a minus into a plus.

Here are some examples of effective people who had to cope with feelings of inferiority.

Helen Keller lost her sight and hearing when she was only nineteen months old, still an infant. She eventually earned a B.A. degree *cum laude* at Radcliffe, became a counselor on international relations for the American Foundation of the Blind, and wrote her famous autobiography, *Story of My Life*.

The author Charles Dickens grew up in poverty. He was forced to work as a child laborer in a factory. He was thin and fearful. An account of his hardship can be read in fictionalized form in his novel *David Copperfield*. (Note that his own initials, C. D., are reversed in the D. C. of the name David Copperfield.) The adult Dickens was one of England's most famous authors, writing, among many other works, *Great Expectations* and *A Christmas Carol*.

The examples could be multiplied by the hundreds. There are countless inspirational stories readily available to you in books and on videotape. What's more, the stories are *true*. It is not imaginary that one can subdue an inferiority complex. Take advantage of this rich treasure, and you will find yourself automatically identifying with the can-do philosophy of effective people.

A PEP TALK

Give Yourself a Pep Talk. Everyone is familiar with the half-time pep talks that coaches give to football teams.

You can make pep talks an object of ridicule and satire, or you can note that they often work. A pep talk is a way of summarizing key facts of a positive nature, of pointing out how a goal can be accomplished, and of replacing a negative motivational state with hope.

You can give yourself a pep talk, when no one else is around, in a mirror. This isn't a bad idea.

A better idea is to write out the talk. Writing forces you to focus your thoughts, to give them greater clarity and definition. Writing also helps you develop a more sustained line of thought than simply thinking about something.

Here is a self-directed pep talk written by Lucy S., a licensed optometrist:

> Here I sit, holder of a doctor of optometry degree. Because I stutter I have allowed myself to be relegated to lab work where I don't have to meet the public. I earn about one-half of what I might make if I could start my own practice and deal with people. But I feel so ashamed of my stuttering.
>
> The truth is that I'm certainly competent enough to meet the public. My inferiority complex about stuttering is just that, a complex. The problem is my self-doubt more than the fact that I sometimes stutter. I have a stutterer's self-image. I see myself as a stutterer instead of as a fluent person. Again, I've learned that so-called fluent persons make all sorts of speech errors all of the time. But they aren't self-conscious about them. I'm going to ask my employer to allow me to see customers one hour a day. I've been thinking about doing this now for three months. The time has arrived. I'm going to talk to him tomorrow morning.
>
> I can do it.
> I can and I will!

As you can see, Lucy's pep talk is highly specific. It deals with a major obstacle that keeps her from moving forward in her life. Your own pep talk should be just as specific. That's why only you can write it. You know yourself and your own private barriers. In your pep talk explore realistic ways to get around an inferiority complex. Tell yourself that where there is a will there really *is* a way. And, like Lucy, tell yourself that the time for action has arrived.

CONTROL

Be Aware That You May Procrastinate as a Way of Maintaining Control of Your Life. Life often presents us with choices we must make, and these choices often involve change. A change from the status quo can be threatening. Naomi has an opportunity for a promotion, and she tells her supervisor, "I'll let you know. I've got to think it over." Nolan has had a close relationship with Gail for a number of years, and she is pressing for marriage. He keeps stalling. Helen is thinking about going to college, but that's all she's doing: thinking. Every time she looks at the college catalog, it makes her tense and anxious. Inez has been married for five years, but she keeps putting off pregnancy, although both she and her husband agree that they want children. In each of these instances the individual is maintaining a sense of control over his or her life by refusing to budge.

The subconscious thought is, "I'll be all right if I can just keep things the way that they are. Now I'm safe. Who knows what risks or potential failures a change might bring?" The individual hugs the present state of affairs in the same way that an infant clings to a favorite blanket.

In each case an inferiority complex acts to block a change in action. Naomi's promotion requires making presentations from time to time, and she thinks, "I'm no good at talking to groups." Nolan doubts that he can live up to Gail's expectations as a breadwinner and potential father. Helen knows that her English and writing skills need improvement and that she will have to take remedial courses. Inez thinks of herself as sickly and wonders if she could survive a pregnancy.

It is important to realize that in each of these cases the inferiority complex is just that, a *complex*. It is a set of *ideas*, not necessarily realistic or correct, that the individual has about his or her own personal attributes. These ideas may have their roots in early childhood experiences, in relatively recent experiences, in things one has been told about oneself by parents or friends, and so forth. But the person may have drawn the wrong conclusions.

Sometimes in this life you have to sail into uncharted waters. You have to let go to some extent. Yes, you evaluate probabilities before you act. But probabilities are not certainties. If you wait for certainties, you will let your golden chances pass you by.

PERSONAL CONSTRUCTS

Modify Your Personal Constructs. George Kelly, a personality theorist, said that a *personal construct* is an idea that you have about yourself. It is called a "construct" because the idea was built by your own mind. Although it is taken by the mind to be reality, it is really a figment of its own imagination. Personal constructs can be positive or negative. Examples of positive ones include "I'm beautiful," or "I'm smart," or "I'm intelligent," or "I'm creative," or "I've got a lot of common sense," or "I'm a loving parent." Before I give examples of negative constructs, let's examine the idea that personal constructs are not necessarily correct. You almost certainly know someone who seems to think and act as if he or she is intelligent. And you have your reservations. You almost certainly know someone who seems to think and act as if he or she is a loving parent. And you don't think so. As you can clearly see, the personal construct *is* in the mind, not in the real world.

Examples of negative personal constructs include, "I'm not pretty," or "Other people are more clever than I am," or "I'm no good at math," or "I can't carry a tune," or "I'm no good at making new friends." Many more examples of negative personal constructs could be given. It is easy for the mind to fabricate negative personal constructs. They are nailed together from the flimsiest of materials. Sometimes a single put-down from a parent in early childhood is enough to plant the seed of a negative personal construct like "I'm not pretty." Sometimes a single bad grade for a semester's work in high school may be enough to draw the conclusion "I'm no good at math." Unfortunately, we are often very suggestible creatures. And the personal construct thrives on suggestion. Once in place, it becomes as solid as an oak door. And it is just as effective a barrier to constructive action.

Negative personal constructs are the stuff from which inferiority complexes are made. Clusters of related negative personal constructs *are* the inferiority complex.

It is important to stress that personal constructs have only psychological, not objective, reality. They are true only if we act on them and make them true. This is correct of both positive and negative constructs. Common sense says that you should replace negative ones with positive ones in order to get on with your life.

Think of personal constructs as fabrications. You are the architect. You can change the blueprint, change what you have built, and change your life.

MAGNIFICATION

Don't Magnify Your Shortcomings. One of the common mental errors made in connection with the personal constructs linked to an inferiority complex is a strong tendency to magnify shortcomings. An attractive woman who is fifteen pounds overweight may say, "I'm as big as a house." A man who is two inches shorter than average may think, "I'm a runt." A college student who really has to study to earn good grades may think, "I'm a blockhead." In each case a relatively modest shortcoming is blown up into a very large one.

Instead think, "I have shortcomings. Who doesn't? Mine are, in general, no worse than anyone else's." State facts to yourself, not sweeping generalizations. It is certainly all right to think, "I'm fifteen pounds overweight," or "I'm two inches shorter than the average male," or "I really have to study to earn good grades." These are reality-oriented statements. And, as such, they are both constructive and useful.

MINIMIZATION

Don't Minimize Your Good Points. Pearl has a lovely figure. When she receives a compliment from a friend, she doesn't say, "Thank you." Instead she discounts it by saying, "Oh, I'm short waisted. It's such a problem when I try on clothes." There are beautiful women who think, "I'm not so pretty. I don't know what people see in me when they say I'm beautiful." There are intelligent people with a lot of ability who think, "I'm a loser. I'm not so smart. I've done fairly well, maybe. But a lot of it is luck." There are creative people who think, "This isn't so hot. I won't show it to anyone." I am reminded of the poet Emily Dickinson. She is believed to be one of the most talented authors who ever lived. However, she minimized her own work and held it back from others. When she died, close to two thousand well-crafted poems were discovered in her files.

Don't puff yourself up and make yourself more than you are. Modesty is, of course, a desirable trait. On the other hand, don't sell yourself short. Be as realistic about your talents and other good points as you are about your shortcomings.

THE INVISIBLE AUDIENCE

Get Rid of the Invisible Audience. The invisible audience consists of parents, siblings, relatives, friends, and acquaintances. They're all watching you. They're not really watching you, of course, but you feel as if they are. They're there in your head like a bunch of ghosts, observing your every action, even your thoughts. In some cases they really are ghosts. Many persons still feel the invisible presence of dead parents who would say something negative about a choice or a line of action if they were still around.

The invisible audience really is just that: invisible. Its members are your own creation. If someone is not actually watching you, then *no one is watching you. You are free. You can do what you want to do without being judged by the standards of others.* I'm not talking about irresponsible or immoral actions. I'm talking about a delay in effective behavior because you imagine that a member of the invisible audience will say, "That's silly," or "That's a bad choice," or, "What do you see in him (or her) as a partner?" or, "I don't really think you know what you're doing."

Dismiss the audience. Imagine yourself saying, "Boo!" Watch the audience vanish.

THE CREATIVE SELF

Discover Your Creative Self. The "creative self" is a very important concept. And so I return to it again. Awareness that you have a creative self is central to your ability to subdue one or several inferiority complexes. It is important to say to yourself, "I have a creative self. I can constructively employ my creative self to change and grow. I can put an inferiority complex in its place and not allow it to control me. An inferiority complex need not cause me to significantly delay my forward progress. It is a block to action only if I allow it to be one."

The discovery of the creative self is the discovery that you can will your own behavior, that you are the agent of action in your life. It is the realization that autonomy, the capacity to pull your own strings and to push your own buttons, is a reality.

≋≋≋   ≋≋≋   ≋≋≋

The Last Word

In this chapter I have demonstrated how you can put the life-enhancing principle of compensation to work. You can turn your minuses into pluses. You don't have to allow an inferiority complex to keep you hesitating and hesitating without effective action.

Key Points to Remember

□— An inferiority complex arises from the frustration of the will to power.

□— An inferiority complex can play a role in procrastination by undermining self-confidence.

□— An inferiority complex is a set of interrelated negative ideas about some aspect of the self.

≋≋≋≋≋≋≋≋≋≋≋≋≋≋≋≋≋≋≋≋≋≋≋≋≋

□— Overcoming an inferiority complex will help you improve your self-esteem.

□— Compensation is an ego defense mechanism that will help you subdue an inferiority complex.

□— Don't be afraid to make mistakes.

□— Become familiar with the biographies of famous people.

□— Give yourself a pep talk.

□— Be aware that you may procrastinate as a way of maintaining control of your life.

□— Modify your personal constructs.

□— Don't magnify your shortcomings.

□— Don't minimize your good points.

□— Get rid of the invisible audience.

□— Discover your creative self.

6 NOBODY IS A BORN PROCRASTINATOR: BREAKING OUT OF A VICIOUS CIRCLE

The author and humorist Mark Twain wrote, "Habit is habit, and not to be flung out of the window by any man, but coaxed downstairs a step at a time."

Chronic procrastination *is* a habit, a "bad" habit. Or to be more precise, chronic procrastination is a self-defeating habit.

In modern psychology, the term *habit* has several meanings such as "a more or less automatic activity" or "a consistent way of behaving." But all of the meanings point to one common assumption: *A habit is learned.* And what has been learned can be unlearned. A habit can be "broken" or modified.

Nobody is a born procrastinator. You did not inherit a "procrastination gene" at birth that gave you this trait. If you have a problem with procrastination, you somehow acquired the difficulty through a chain of experiences and consequences that entrenched the habit.

This brings us back to Mark Twain's observation. A "bad" habit deserves our respect because it is a formidable opponent. As he suggests, we seldom can break a habit directly by brute willpower. Instead, we have to break it indirectly by well-known habit-breaking methods. Using Twain's language, we have to "coax" the habit down the stairs until we can show it the door and shut it out of our lives.

The procrastination habit is a self-defeating, vicious circle. This chapter will show you effective ways to break out of the circle.

Breaking Out

Personal application of the following self-directed coping strategies and practical tips will free you, in time, from the habit of procrastination. They can all be readily employed in daily living. But be patient. Chronic procrastination is a personality trait and, as such, resists change. But *small* changes applied on a regular basis can gradually unravel the trait.

HABIT ANALYSIS

Make a Habit Analysis. A habit analysis is a kind of psychological map of your procrastination habit. It helps you to see the outlines of a behavioral pattern in bold relief. In the same way that sonar can display the hidden shape of an iceberg, a habit analysis can bring forth the key factors in a self-defeating habit.

At this point let's take an important conceptual step. Let's make a distinction between your procrastination Habit with a capital H and the smaller habits that make it up. In other words, in making a habit analysis, we will follow the "divide and conquer" rule. We will undermine the big bad Habit by breaking it down into a set of less formidable small habits.

<u>Get a set of index cards. On the front of each card note a single procrastination habit</u>. Don't expect to capture all of the individual habits on cards in one day. Just observe your own behavior for a week or so, and when you can, jot down what has been noted.

Here is a portion of a habit analysis made by Carl G., a college student:

> *Card 1*. Whenever I'm supposed to study history and political science I find every excuse in the world to avoid doing so.

Card 2. I'm always taking books to the library late and paying big fines I can't afford.

Card 3. I ought to write home more often. Sometimes I let weeks go by without sending Mom and Dad a line. I feel guilty about neglecting them so much.

Here is a portion of a habit analysis made by Amelia B., a single mother and a nurse:

Card 1. I set aside Saturday mornings to vacuum and dust. But I call my sister before I start and sometimes waste an hour on the phone. Then I don't feel like doing any housework.

Card 2. I often leave for work with a sink full of undone dishes. And I hate this. I *hate* coming home to a mess.

Card 3. I don't put gas in the car when I'm supposed to. I often let the tank run dangerously low. I've run out of gas twice in the past few months.

Card 4. I always say that I'm going to spend "quality time" with the kids, but never seem to get around to it.

Card 5. I tell myself I'm busy and always on the run, but the truth is I just plain goof off a lot. Last week I spent four hours rereading *Gone With the Wind* when I had all kinds of important errands to run. I felt *awful* while I was reading. I was feeling too guilty about all of the undone things.

RANKING

Make a Ranking of the Cards. Put the "weakest" specific habit on the top of the set, and put the "strongest" habit on the bottom. The weakest habit is the one that you yourself perceive as being the easiest one to modify or break. Work on that one first for a few days until you have achieved some degree of success. Then turn to the next one in the stack.

For example, in Amelia's case, she worked on Card 2. She hated coming home from work to a sink full of dirty dishes, and didn't really mind cleaning up all that much, so she decided that this individual habit might be readily attacked.

BRAINSTORMING

Brainstorm Solutions. As you read and reread the procrastination habits on the front of the cards, explore what strategies and interventions you can realistically apply to unbalance the habit. In this search you are not without assets. Use this book as a source of ideas. This chapter has a number of them. Also, turn to other chapters for practical hints. Jot down on the back of the appropriate card the self-directed strategy, or strategies, that seem likely to work.

The rest of this chapter focuses on specific habit-breaking skills that you can either place on the back of a habit-analysis card or immediately apply.

PREMACK'S PRINCIPLE

Apply Premack's Principle. Premack's principle is also known at an informal level in psychology as *The Grandparents' Rule.* You'll see how it is one of the most important principles of behavioral self-modification ever discovered.

Working with rats, David Premack, an experimental psychologist at the University of California at Santa Barbara, was well aware of the long-standing observation that rats will run at length in a freely rotating cage. They receive no reinforcement or obvious reward for doing this. The behavior is self-reinforcing or self-rewarding. In informal terms, rats appear to "like" to run in spinning cages.

These familiar observations have led behavioral scientists to postulate the existence of an *activity drive*, an inborn drive to move around and engage in spontaneous actions. This appears to be true not only of rats, but also of human beings.

Think of yourself being forced to endure a long wait in a doctor's office. Can you just sit in a chair and stare straight ahead for a half hour? Don't you at least have to cross and uncross your legs? It is even more likely that you will change your position in the chair, get up and check your standing with the receptionist, try to read a magazine, walk outside of the office for a few minutes, and so forth. In brief, *you are restless* and only *activity* can make you feel a little better. We obviously don't need to look to rat studies to convince ourselves that we have an activity drive. A little introspection reveals that it is clearly there.

Premack wondered if he could use the activity drive to reinforce another behavior, one that had no self-reinforcing value. He set up an apparatus that contained a lever. If the rat pressed the lever, it obtained the opportunity to run for a fixed unit of time (for example, five minutes). The lever released a brake, and the rat could enter the rotating cage via a tunnel connecting the cage to the box containing the lever. The rat had free access to both areas, and, with experience and learning, became an "enthusiastic" lever presser. Be sure you note at this point that lever pressing has little or no self-reinforcing value.

Let's apply all of this to you and daily living, making the bridge from the rat world to the human world. There is something that you have no intrinsic interest in doing. It, like lever pressing for the rat, has no built-in psychological value. In ordinary language, we say it is behavior that we don't "like" to do or "want" to do. In Premack's language, he called such behavior *low-probability behaviors*. This designation is useful because it allows us to readily target such behaviors in ourselves.

There is something that you "like" to do. This is *a high-probability behavior*. Now we have arrived at one of the important keys to breaking specific procrastination habits. *Make the opportunity to engage in high-probability behaviors contingent upon the performance of low-probability behaviors.* That's it in a nutshell. If you fully understand and apply this key, you will find yourself successfully fighting procrastination on many fronts.

Carl tends to avoid studying, puts it off to the last minute, and ends up cramming for tests. He rents two or three videotapes at a time, and spends pointless hours watching action-adventure and science-fiction movies. Watching videotapes is a high-probability behavior. If he watches videotapes *first* and *then* studies, he tends to study less and less, consequently reinforcing his procrastination habit. However, if he promises himself that he will study first and then watch a videotape, he will find that he will eventually study more and more and watch videotapes less and less. (Easier said than done, you may be thinking. More about this point later.)

If Amelia promises herself that she will do important chores or run errands *before* she reads a novel, then she will reinforce "responsible" behavior and extinguish "goof-off" behavior. Indeed, goof-off behavior acquires a very important role when Premack's principle is used. It is like fighting fire with fire. The very behavior that is causing a problem is used to extinguish its own blaze.

Premack's principle is sound. There's no doubt about it. However, getting yourself to apply the principle—countering the "easier said than done" observation—requires some specific skills. Let's take a look at these skills.

TASK ORIENTATION

Specify a Responsible Behavior in Terms of a Well-Defined Task, Not Time. I call this a task-orientation approach versus a time-orientation approach. Assume that Carl says to himself, "I'm going to study history for an hour." Now he has made himself a prisoner of time. He doesn't enjoy studying history and he keeps looking at his watch. "Only twenty minutes has gone by," he groans. "It feels more like two hours."

I know a man who as a child was required to practice the violin for an hour every afternoon. He comments today, "That hour always seemed to last forever." We want to free ourselves from these kinds of experiences. We don't want time to be a psychological straitjacket.

DEFINING THE TASK

Define a Task in Both a Limited Way and a Concrete Way. In the application of Premack's principle, it is essential to avoid vague, nebulous statements about what you "ought" to do and "should" do. Carl says he should study more history and political science. Amelia says she should spend more quality time with her children.

Carl needs to zero in on the vague phrase "study more" and translate it into a concrete task such as, "Study four pages in chapter 5 of the history textbook." Now he has before him a well-defined, limited task. Now "studying more" does not seem so formidable.

Similarly, Amelia needs to translate "spending quality time" into something more specific. Lately her eight-year-old daughter, Debbie, has discovered checkers, and asks her mother from time to time to play a game with her. Amelia usually puts Debbie off with vague promises such as, "We'll play when I have more time." In defining her task, Amelia can say to herself, or write on the back of a habit analysis card, "I'll play at least three games of checkers a week with Debbie."

I am well aware that playing checkers with a child should in some ideal world not be a "task." Nonetheless, even a loving parent may perceive it as such because of lack of actual interest in the game itself. Therefore, even such seemingly natural behaviors as playing with one's own children may require the application of self-modification of behavior skills.

Thousands of well-meaning people are forever telling themselves that they should exercise more. But what does "exercise more" mean? A vapid generalization has to be translated into a well-defined task. The individual has to say something such as, "I will take four brisk twenty-minute walks a week" or "I will use my exercise bicycle for three thirty-minute sessions each week."

I don't enjoy doing yard work. As long as I define the task in this way I don't do much yard work. "Yard work" is a vague ghost that haunts many a homeowner. (Of course, I understand that some people like yard work and love to garden. This paragraph is not addressed to them.) Now that I've grown up a little I say to myself, "I intend to fix those three clogged sprinklers Saturday morning," or "I am going to fertilize the lawn Friday afternoon." The huge specter of "yard work" is recast into a shrunken, manageable form.

BEHAVIORAL CONTRACTING

Make a Behavioral Contract Between Your Adult Self and Your Child Self. One of the behavior modification skills that is taught in workshops on child rearing is behavioral contracting. *Behavioral contracting* calls for a negotiation between parent and child, for the "making of a deal." A parent says, "If you do your arithmetic homework, then you can call your friend Susan. OK?" If the child says, "Oh, Mom, let me call Susan first, then I promise I'll do my homework," the parent must say, "No. That won't do." Then the parent must try to make the contract again. The contract exists when the child says something like, "Oh, OK." When the contract is made and held to, it has the effect of strengthening the child's low-probability behavior (doing homework) and weakening the child's high-probability behavior (talking to a friend on the phone).

In the same way that a behavioral contract is made between a parent and child, you can make a contract, as already suggested, between your adult self and your child self. Carl's adult self promises his child self that if he studies four pages of chapter 5, he then can watch a videotape he has rented. He can watch the videotape and really enjoy it, *without guilt*, because he has earned the right to watch it. If instead he procrastinates and watches the videotape before studying, he will feel vaguely guilty and generally ineffective. His pleasure is destroyed by the knowledge that he is being irresponsible.

Amelia makes a behavioral contract that says that if her adult self plays checkers with her eight-year-old daughter, then her child self can read ten pages of a novel without guilt.

In the beginning, it is advantageous to put the behavioral contract *in writing*, to make it a semiformal agreement between your adult ("responsible") self and your child ("irresponsible") self. (Only two or three lines are necessary.) There is something about putting contracts on paper that produces a tendency to follow through and complete the deal.

IMMEDIATE GRATIFICATION

Give Yourself Immediate Gratification After You Engage in the Low-Probability Behavior. Experiments on learning in both animals and human beings have revealed that new learning is acquired much more effectively if it receives swift reinforcement. So right away, without delay, allow yourself the pleasure of engaging in your designated high-probability behavior after completing your self-assigned task.

DURATION OF THE GRATIFICATION

Place a Time Limit Ahead of Time on the Duration of the Gratification. As you were reading about Carl and his efforts to study, this objection may have occurred to you: "But it might take Carl only fifteen minutes or twenty minutes to study the four pages he defined as his task. Then he might watch the videotape for an hour and a half. Isn't this pretty inefficient?"

Of course, the answer is that it *is* inefficient. In the beginning, just to get low-probability behavior going at all, it is perhaps a good idea to allow oneself a large gratification. But as low-probability behavior makes gains and begins to offer less resistance, it is also possible, in turn, to place time limits on the gratification associated with high-probability behavior. Consequently, Carl might, after a week or two, promise himself that he will watch one-half of a videotape, study four more pages, and then watch the rest of the videotape.

An eventual procrastination-avoidance skill is to *alternate* between low-probability and high-probability behaviors in such a way that the time spent in reinforcing low-probability behavior shrinks to acceptable levels. You will find that one of the advantages of applying Premack's principle is that you will spend more and more time accomplishing responsible tasks and less and less time goofing off.

The Last Word

This chapter has focused on *short-term procrastination*, the avoidance of "small" behaviors that are seen as either unpleasant or burdensome chores. *Long-term procrastination*, in contrast, is the avoidance of taking the necessary steps involved in making personal dreams and life goals come true. Dealing with both kinds of procrastination is important.

We make large gains by taking small steps. Remember what the Chinese sage Lao-tzu said, "A journey of a thousand miles begins with a single step." Learning to deal with short-term procrastination can help you successfully complete "the thousand-mile journey" that will bring you closer to your most cherished aspirations.

Key Points to Remember

□⚊ Procrastination is a habit. A habit is learned. And what has been learned can be unlearned.

□⚊ A habit can be broken by the application of well-known habit-breaking methods.

□⚊ Make a *habit analysis*, a kind of psychological map of your procrastination habit.

□⚊ Break your procrastination Habit with a capital H into the smaller habits that make it up.

□⚊ Make a ranking of your habit analysis cards. Work on the "weakest" habits first.

□⚊ Apply Premack's principle. Remember the key to the principle: Make the opportunity to engage in high-probability behaviors contingent upon the performance of low-probability behaviors.

□⚊ Specify a responsible behavior in terms of a well-defined task, not time.

□⚊ Define a task in both a limited way and a concrete way.

□⚊ Make a behavioral contract between your adult self and your child self. Put your contract *in writing*.

□⚊ Give yourself immediate gratification after you engage in a low-probability behavior.

□⚊ Place a time limit ahead of time on the duration of the gratification.

□⚊ This chapter has focused on ways to cope with *short-term procrastination*.

7 REACHING YOUR GOALS AND DREAMS: ARE YOU RUNNING ON THE WRONG ROAD?

One of the best ways to avoid procrastination is to ask yourself: "Where am I going?"

Dwelling on the past, on its slights, misfortunes, abuses, and deprivations, won't get you anywhere. When I was an adolescent I once rented a speedboat for an hour at Lake Arrowhead, California. As I raced about the lake with my date I had a wonderful sense of freedom. I could go any direction I wanted to go. I looked at the wake of the boat. It was large and impressive. Then I thought, "But it isn't pushing me. *I* steer the ship." From time to time I return to that image, and I think, "The past is like the wake of the boat. It's *behind* the boat. It's gone. The past doesn't cause the present any more than the wake of the boat pushes it on its way. My inner will can steer my life in accordance with my desires in the same way I was able to steer the boat."

By focusing on the future, not the past, we rise above the past and free ourselves from it.

We are purposive creatures. Ask a child why he or she is walking to the market. The child answers, "To buy a quart of milk for Mom." Note that even in this small case a purpose has been stated. The child has given an answer that orients toward the future, not the past.

To dwell on the past is to stay mired in psychological mud. It is normal and natural for us to raise our eyes from the mud and to gaze upon the stars. In this case the stars are metaphors for your goals and dreams.

Abraham Maslow, a principal founder of humanistic psychology, said that we all have an inborn need for self-actualization. We have a strong desire to become the self we were meant to become. We crave to make the most of our talents and our potentialities. However, if you have been sidetracked into a vocation or a style of life that is leading you away from becoming the person you were meant to be, you are selling yourself short.

Procrastination is one symptom of living a life that is not sufficiently self-actualizing.

Paradoxically, excessive busyness can also be a symptom of a lack of self-actualization. Keeping yourself overly active in a kind of nervous froth doesn't, on the surface, look like procrastination. But, in a very real sense, it is. You are procrastinating about the things that really count. You are using irrelevant activity as a kind of psychological stuffing to fill up an emotional emptiness. If this is the case, you have got to slow down and take a hard look at your life. A German proverb asks, "What is the use of running if you're on the wrong road?" Ask yourself this question, and listen to the answer that arises from within.

We are creatures that need meaning in life. The search for meaning is also oriented toward the future. The normal person finds meaning in emotional closeness with a partner, in raising children, and in giving something of worth in the form of products or services to others. The goals that have special meaning to you are called *values*. It is important to know what these values are and to actually work toward them. You won't tend to procrastinate if you know where you are going and why.

Making Practical Applications

The following suggestions will help you focus your energies in such a way that you can more effectively meet both your need for self-actualization and your need for meaning. If you believe that you are on the right road, you won't want to waste your time procrastinating. Instead, you will be enthusiastic and want to make efficient use of your time.

DEFINING GOALS

Define at Least One Major Goal and a Minor Goal Associated With It. A major goal is a long-term goal. It may take months or years to reach it. A minor goal is a subgoal, and may be achieved in a relatively short time. It is rewarding to attain a subgoal. The positive psychological payoff that flows from its attainment keeps you on the pathway toward the major goal.

It is a good idea to put your goals in writing.

Hal D. defined his goals as follows: "I've been an amateur songwriter since I was sixteen. But I've never sent anything to a publisher. I must have fifty or more songs that I think have some merit. A major goal is to get a song published. A minor goal is to make at least one demonstration tape with a lead sheet and actually send it in to a publisher."

Rosalind S. defined her goals as follows: "I work for a certified public accountant as an accounting clerk. A major goal is to become a CPA myself. A minor goal is to successfully complete Accounting 101 in an evening class at my local community college."

Shanelle A. defined her goals as follows: "A major goal for me is to improve my relationship with my twenty-four-year-old daughter. A minor goal is to avoid criticizing the way she is raising my four-year-old grandson the next time I visit her."

Jordon H. defined his goals as follows: "I've always thought I could sing. A major goal is to have at least a part-time career as a singer. A minor goal is to try out for a part in the local community production of *Fiddler on the Roof.*"

Verna L. defined her goals as follows: "I get such a kick out of watching tennis tournaments. My dream is not to play professional tennis, but just to play. That's my major goal: to play tennis with a modicum of ability. My minor goal is to sign up for the group tennis lessons given by the city recreational department."

VISUALIZING

Visualize Your Goal. It will give your goal-directed activity quite a boost if you can visualize your goal. There are many ways to do this. Zelma D. wanted to lose weight. She clipped several photographs of women with attractive bodies from magazines and taped these to the refrigerator door.

Going back to Jordon H., he enjoys cartooning. He drew a picture of himself singing in a musical production. Even if you can't draw well, you can try making some sort of picture of what you want to do or accomplish. Even if your final production looks like a child's drawing, so what? Children's drawings often have enormous power.

Close your eyes and try to *see* yourself reaching a major goal. Daydream what you want to be. This is a constructive way to use fantasy in your life.

Visualization of a goal tends to trigger the activity of our natural forward-looking tendencies. As already noted, we are purposive creatures. Our sense of purpose is greatly nurtured if we can see in our mind's eye where we are going. It is like the clearing away of a fog. You have been driving along slowly, with hesitation. Now with good vision, you start zipping along. Visualization helps you to clear away mental fog.

THE TIME MACHINE

Take a Time Machine Trip. Using your creative imagination, take a time machine trip into the future. Actually, you want to take two trips. The first trip should be into a future in which you have procrastinated and not actually worked toward your goals. The second trip should be into a future in which you have used time effectively and have attained your goals.

The idea for using a time machine trip as a guidance technique came to me when I was counseling Margo F., a young mother who was thinking of becoming a medical doctor. She was recently divorced, a community college student, and the mother of two young children. Becoming a medical doctor seemed to be an impossible dream. She wanted to know what to do. On the one hand, it would seem very tempting to say, "Now, look, Margo. Be realistic. This is really a far-fetched idea. You have two kids to raise. You'll almost certainly neglect them if you pursue this particular academic track." And so on.

On the other hand, who am I to say? Maybe she will inspire her children by being a role model. Maybe she will be a better mother if she is happy and fulfilled. Who knows?

Carl Rogers, the father of client-centered therapy, would have answered, "Margo knows." Margo is the expert on her own life, not me. But the therapist can provide a structure that will help Margo *discover* her own right road.

So I induced a guided fantasy and described a time machine. The time machine looked like a huge plastic egg sitting on a tripod. It had a comfortable chair and a dial marked with years running into the future. Margo entered the machine and I suggested that she take herself ten years into the future, a future in which she *had not* worked toward becoming a medical doctor. At this point she took over the fantasy. She described a future that was deprived and unhappy. She lived in a threadbare house and eked out a living at a job she didn't like. Her children were thin and moody. You might object that this was only a fantasy, that it might not have turned out the way she described it. True, but this was Margo's image of how things would turn out if she didn't follow her dream. And images have a way of becoming self-fulfilling prophecies.

I suggested that she come back to the present and take a second trip ten years into the future, a future in which she had worked toward becoming a medical doctor. Again, Margo took over the fantasy. Now she lived in a small, but attractive apartment. Life was bright and full. She and her children had a good relationship. She had completed her internship and she was planning to do resident training in internal medicine.

When she opened her eyes and we discussed the two trips, she told me that the first trip was poorly visualized and had a dismal quality to it. The second trip was clearly visualized, and it glowed in her mind. It vibrated with reality. She told me that she was certain that her calling in life was to become a medical doctor.

I don't know all of the details. But through a combination of family help, government loans and grants, and some scholarship money, Margo was able to become a physician.

OPTIONS

Consider Your Options. You are traveling a life road. It may seem to you that there is no exit from this road, that there is no way to cross over to another better road. This is seldom the case. Life is full of options. However, you may need to do some reflecting in order to discover what they are. Take some time out to think things through. Again, it is a good idea to put your thoughts in writing. Describe the life road you are on as you presently see it. Then write down one or several options, several possible exits that you see as distinct possibilities.

Gary L. had been a claims adjuster for a large insurance company for seven years. He was good at his job and had benefits. With the responsibility of a family, he didn't feel he could afford the luxury of quitting. He felt trapped in a job that seemed to him to be overly demanding and emotionally unrewarding. It was very painful for him to think of himself traveling down a life road in which his vocation remained claims adjuster for a total of twenty

years or more. In considering his options, Gary rediscovered the fact that he had always been a very talented public speaker. In high school and college he had won several awards. He decided to make an application at a local community college to teach a speech class at night. He was turned down. They had too many speech teachers already.

Then Gary, still exploring alternatives, learned that a local state college had an extension program, again offered mostly at night. He conferred with a coordinator for the program and found out that it was possible to teach classes on a contingency basis. The college would give him 25 percent of the gross revenue. His first class was a small success. His second class he promoted to some extent on his own. He sent a mailer to a selected list. He contacted several local newspapers, and short interviews were printed. He was invited to be a guest on a local radio talk show. There was a large turnout for his second class. Gary now has a successful public speaking business of his own. He teaches at five different colleges, mostly evenings and Saturdays. He offers his services as a professional master of ceremonies and is paid well for his work. He was able to quit his job as a claims adjuster.

Nell D. was a machinist. Although she had excellent training for this skilled trade, she was convinced, after four years on the job, that she was in the wrong line of work. The single mother of four children, she was sure that she was stuck on the wrong road. But she felt that it would be irresponsible to quit her job. Considering her options, she rediscovered the fact that she liked flower arranging. She usually thought of it as a pleasant hobby, certainly not something that could become a career. Now she began to think about the large number of florist shops in her area. She made applications for part-time work, and one florist gave her on-the-job training. Nell's talents quickly came to the fore, and she was soon working many extra hours.

Nell's employer, a middle-aged man, was interested in semiretirement. He was looking for a responsible partner. Nell was the perfect candidate. She had some money saved and was able to make a down payment on half of the business. The employer, now a partner, took an unsecured note for the balance that she owed. This was several years ago, and the note has been paid off. Nell and her partner have a thriving business, and she is at last in a line of work that brings both emotional satisfaction and financial reward.

LIKING WHAT YOU DO

Be Sure That You Like What You Do for a Career. It might seem like a luxury, an unnecessary frill, to like what you do for a career. Perhaps you are trying to be tough-minded. "As long as I put bread on the table, the nature of my job is unimportant." However, reflect on the saying "A human being does not live by bread alone." If you just work, and think of your daily effort as a kind of miserable hoop-jumping behavior that has no meaning, joy, or value other than bringing you a paycheck, you'll never make a real success out of what you are doing. Not liking what you do can be a real factor in procrastination. You resist your daily tasks. Perhaps you arrive late or are absent a lot. You use all of your sick leave days although you aren't really sick.

Make a distinction between a job and a vocation. A job is just something you do to survive. All of us have had jobs. Sometimes we have to take a job just to get by. However, think of the job not as a dead end, but as a stepping stone on the pathway to your true vocation. A vocation is a calling in life. It is meaningful. The work you do in connection with it is self-actualizing.

Maybe procrastination in connection with distasteful employment is trying to tell you something. Seemingly unnecessary delays and self-defeating avoidance tactics can be ways that your subconscious mind sends an important message to your conscious mind. Don't remain stuck for years and years in a job that you really dislike. You may think you're being practical. But nothing, in the long run, could be more impractical.

TARGET DATES

Set Target Dates. It is a good idea to establish a desirable date of completion for a project. Sometimes, of course, this is done for you by an employer. If a target date is not imposed from the outside, impose it yourself, from inside. Make the date specific. "I plan to have all of my house-hold bills paid by Saturday afternoon." "I am going to have all of my lawn sprinklers unclogged and working by Tuesday afternoon." These examples refer to relatively modest projects. Larger projects require even more commitment. Consequently, target dates become more significant as the project itself becomes more significant. "I expect to complete the book report for my history class by November 10." "I plan to take a trip to England in the summer of 1998."

Setting target dates automatically mobilizes your resources and sets up a planning process. You begin to think about how to use your time effectively. The date creates an *internal press*, an inner psychological "push" that keeps you going and sticking to the task. Although you have given birth to the target date yourself, it takes on a reality of its own. In fact there can be a danger in this. A target date can become a deadline. The difference between a target date and a deadline is both subtle and subjective. They are, of course, both quite similar. A target date is *desirable*. It is perceived as a goal, something you would like to attain if practical. A deadline, on the other hand, is perceived as a *must*. The unspoken attitude that goes with it is that something awful will happen if the task is not completed by the date. There is an underlying feeling of doom and potential catastrophe. The problem is in the word *dead*. No one will die if the "deadline" is not met. It is important to realize that something can go wrong even if you don't procrastinate. You might get ill. You might have unexpected responsibilities thrust on you. If so, you have to modify your target date. The important point is to distinguish between circumstances that are genuinely beyond your control, that actually *force* you to change a target date, and convenient rationalizations that allow you to procrastinate.

A target date is a positive force in your life. It is something you *want* to actualize. A deadline is a negative force. It is perceived as a burden you are carrying. Think in terms of target dates, not deadlines.

KNOCKING ON DOORS

Knock on Many Doors. We are all familiar with the saying "It's not what you know, it's who you know." The implication is that if you have relatives or friends in high places, they will set up easy opportunities for you. No one denies that this is true in a few cases. However, in the vast majority of cases you have to create your own opportunities. Actually, if you knock on many doors, you will eventually know a lot of people who can help you. In a sense, you make the old saying come true. The "who" becomes a person you have gotten to know from your own initiative.

There are certain fields of endeavor where we use the term *break in.* We speak of "breaking into show business," "breaking into the movies," "breaking into advertising," "breaking into modeling," and so forth. The "break in" language is used because beginners see themselves as outsiders who have no open door into what seems to be a charmed circle. If you think of the circle as a magical barrier, you may just walk away and make no realistic effort at all. However, if you will be persistent and "knock on many doors," you will often be rewarded for your efforts. You will become a familiar name or a familiar face. Often you will be given a chance, a small opportunity. If you actually have talent, or whatever ability is required, it will be recognized. Small opportunities will lead to larger ones, and you will have "broken in."

In order to illustrate the importance of the above process, allow me to briefly relate the story of just one person. He was an East Coast dentist who wanted to write novels. A number of publishers rejected his first novel. Discouraged, he and his wife published the novel with some money she had inherited. The project was a financial flop.

He kept writing, sending his manuscripts into publishers, and knocking on many doors. At one point he was told by an eminent editor that he should stick to dentistry and forget writing. He was told that he had no talent. The would-be author thought to himself, "Who's he to tell me that I can't write?" And he vowed anew to make his personal dream come true.

He visited the West for the first time when he was an adult. He was the guest of a famous buffalo hunter. Fascinated by the large expanses of land, his imagination was stimulated. After repeated submissions, a publisher accepted *Riders of the Purple Sage*. Released in 1912, it became one of the most popular Western novels ever written. Success begat success, and he wrote many Western novels. He sold screen rights to his novels for $50,000 each during the Great Depression, when $50,000 was worth $500,000 or more in today's money.

His name was Zane Grey.

Zane Grey didn't know anybody when he started out. He was laughed at. "What does an East Cost dentist know about the West?" But he knocked on many doors and "broke in" by his own efforts.

YOUR LIFE SCRIPT

Rewrite Your Life Script. Transactional analysis, a theory of personality associated with the psychiatrist Eric Berne, asserts that people have Life Scripts. (Note that in transactional analysis it is a convention to capitalize certain key words.) A Script is "written" in childhood. It states in a kind of general way what direction your life will take. The Script is based on your prepubertal experiences, experiences that suggest you will be a Winner, a Loser, or an Also Ran. Most people have an Also Ran Script. Unconsciously, this dictates that they will not be complete failures, but they will also prohibit themselves from becoming very successful. A smaller percentage of people have a Loser Script. This dictates that they will be self-defeating, self-destructive, or both. And then there are people who have a Winning Script. This dictates that they will be self-actualizing, discover meaning in life, and attain their most important goals.

The theory of transactional analysis steadfastly insists that you can use your adult self to rewrite a Script. You may be acting out a Script written by a prepubertal child. It is possible to look at your behavior and your decisions and to say, "I want to rewrite the Script. I'm obviously living out an Also Ran Script, so I'm going to revise my plan. I'm writing a new Script, a Winning Script."

Write a one- or two-page description of the direction your life will take if you follow a Winning Script. Make this description the basis of your revised Life Script.

Note that procrastination is a negative factor, one that contributes to Also Ran and Loser Scripts. When you read over your Winning Script, you will see that you have automatically left out procrastination.

THE WILL

Believe in the Power of the Will. It is easy to lose faith in the power of the will. People often see themselves as the victims of emotional conflicts and bad habits. If you believe you are a victim of these forces, you will be. On the other hand, if you believe in the power of the will, you can rise above negative psychological factors.

The doctrine of *determinism* in philosophy and psychology teaches that all behavior is caused. It is caused by genes, blood chemistry, the activity of the brain, motives, memories, and learned tendencies. This seems obvious. Or is it? If you accept this point of view entirely, where is there room for free will? Determinism teaches us that we are high-level robots, but robots all the same.

On the other hand, the doctrine of *voluntarism* in philosophy and psychology teaches that behavior can be willed. We can always take a stand against negative conditions. We can make real choices. This also seems to be apparent because we day-to-day *experience* ourselves as willing our behavior.

Which point of view is the correct one? There is probably some truth in both viewpoints, so you don't really have to make a choice. The issue is still a lively one in philosophical circles.

I can tell you this, however. People who believe in the power of their own will have a strong point in their favor. A strong sense of autonomy is an important factor in mental health. In view of the fact that, from a philosophical standpoint, neither position can be rigidly asserted, you might as well live your life not as a determined creature, but as one that has free will. A genuine belief in free will tends to generate its own reality.

The author William Ernest Henley lost a leg when he was a child. After overcoming many hardships, he wrote a poem called "Invictus," a Latin word for "Unconquered." The last two lines are famous and well worth memorizing. Recite them to yourself when you want to give your willpower an extra boost, when you are tempted to put off until tomorrow what you would be better off doing today. They are:

> I am the master of my fate;
> I am the captain of my soul.

MR. MEANT-TO

Memorize Mr. Meant-To. Below you will find a poem by an anonymous author. Like the lines from "Invictus," if you commit "Mr. Meant-To" to memory and mentally recite the poem at moments when you are tempted to procrastinate, you will find it a powerful ally in your efforts to get down to brass tacks and actually get things done.

> Mr. Meant-To has a comrade,
> And his name is Didn't-Do;
> Have you ever chanced to meet them?
> Did they ever call on you?
> These two fellows live together
> In the house of Never-Win,
> And I'm told that it is haunted
> By the ghost of Might-Have-Been.

The Last Word

As noted in the chapter opening, we are purposive beings. If your goals and dreams are vague or nonexistent, procrastination will be a problem. This is because you have no real desire to be engaged in the tasks or to do the work, required to arrive at a questionable destination. This chapter has shown how to (1) define your dreams and goals and (2) initiate constructive behavior toward them

Key Points to Remember

- By focusing on the future, not the past, we rise above the past and free ourselves from it.

- Procrastination is one symptom of living a life that is not sufficiently self-actualizing

- We are beings that need meaning in life. Goals with special meaning are called *values*.

- Define at least one major goal and a minor goal associated with it.

- Visualize your goal.

- Take a time machine trip.

- Consider your options.

- Be sure that you like what you do for a career.

- Set target dates.

- Knock on many doors.

- Rewrite your life script.

- Believe in the power of the will.

- Memorize "Mr. Meant-To."

8 INTERPERSONAL ASPECTS: ARE YOU HURTING YOURSELF OR SOMEONE ELSE?

Other people.

Who are they?

They are everyone but you. The world has several billion other people, but only one you.

The other people in your life that have paramount importance are called *significant others*. They consist primarily of your parents, siblings, your partner, and your children. Grandparents, other relatives, friends, employers, supervisors, coworkers, peers, and friends may also play an important part in your life. The way in which you interact with people who are an important part in your life often plays a major role in procrastination.

For example, you may procrastinate in order to strike back at someone else, to hurt him or her when you feel frustrated or otherwise offended by the other person. There will be more about this point later.

Interpersonal behavior is behavior that involves interactions with other people. Its two principal components are the interpersonal stimulus and the interpersonal response. The *interpersonal stimulus* is manifest when you make an attempt to elicit a response from someone else. For example, you say, "Good morning" to someone. The *interpersonal response* is manifest when the other person reacts to the stimulus you have presented. For example, the other person says, "And good morning to you." Or the other person might say, "What's good about it?" In either case, the other person has provided you with a response.

A really important factor to consider is the interpersonal interaction. The *interpersonal interaction* is the living pattern created by the stimulus and response. It is the outcome of the give and take. If the response to your cheerful "Good morning" is an equally cheerful one, the interpersonal interaction has been positive. And you will probably feel refreshed by it. If the response to your cheerful "Good morning" is an unexpectedly grouchy one, the interpersonal interaction has been negative. And you will probably feel deflated by it.

Interpersonal interactions have a lot to do with the way we feel about life and living. They also have a lot to do with whether or not we will procrastinate.

Coping Strategies

The coping strategies listed below are all designed to help you improve the quality of your interpersonal behavior. They are practical skills aimed specifically at a tendency to procrastinate.

PASSIVE BEHAVIOR

Reject the Temptation to Be Passive. Another person asks you to do something. You don't want to do it. You don't think you should do it. You resent being asked at all. And what do you do? You say, "Oh, all right." You have just made a contract to do what you have been asked to do.

Now what do you do? You take your sweet time. Or you "forget" to do whatever it is. Or you don't do a good job. Or you work at a very slow rate. Or you find little excuses that allow you to postpone the required actions.

You have been passive. You have been too agreeable in a misguided effort to be a "nice, likable person." But your passivity has led to passive-aggressive behavior. *Passive-aggressive* behavior is behavior that is agreeable and cooperative on the surface, but negative and hostile at a latent level. The truth is that you are paying back the other person for presenting an interpersonal stimulus that you find offensive.

When you are asked to do something that you genuinely don't think you should do, stand your ground. Don't turn hostile and say something such as, "What is wrong with you? Don't you know better? I can't see why you're asking me to do that! That's your job!" If the other person's affection or good will is important to you, then a hostile response can only have long-term adverse consequences.

Instead, say in a firm voice something such as, "I really don't think I want to do that." Give a sound reason why, if you want to, but don't launch into an elaborate defense.

WHO'S THE BOSS?

Play by the Boss's Rules. Perhaps you objected to the prior principle. If an employer, a supervisor, or a master sergeant makes a request or gives an order, you don't have the luxury of saying no. In such instances, of course, play by the boss's rules. You are in his or her field of power, and it is inappropriate for you to think that you can call the shots. Unfortunately, many people in the workplace resent being told what to do, and manifest passive-aggressive behavior. Tell yourself, in selected situations, "I'm going to play by the boss's rules, not mine." Make a positive change in your attitude, and you will be less likely to procrastinate.

However, in the case of the first principle, I was referring to relationships with significant others. If a wife asks her husband to do something, or vice versa, the question arises, "Who's the boss?" Obviously, in the case of a marriage, neither the husband nor the wife is "the boss." Consequently, it is appropriate to negotiate when requests are imposed upon you that you really want to reject.

SOCIAL ROLES

Avoid Posturing Social Roles. A *social role* is a part we play in life, somewhat in the same way that an actor plays a part in a play. A *functional* social role is one that makes a contribution to the family or to the larger community. Familiar functional social roles are parent, teacher, healer, friend, and so forth. A *posturing* social role is one that has a selfish goal. They are the masks we wear when we want to (1) get our own way and (2) hide our true feelings and motives.

The *Slowpoke* is a role used by an individual who seems to be set on slow-motion time. (Note that it is a convention to capitalize a social role in order to distinguish it from the actual person who uses the role.) He or she takes "forever" to get anything done. The Slowpoke's mode of procrastinating is to draw everything out, to take a lot of breaks, to work at a snail's pace. This, of course, sends a message to others. A spouse may be covertly saying, "I hate to cook and clean house." In a different aspect of marriage, another spouse may be saying, "I really don't want to get dressed to go to a party made up of your old friends." An adolescent may be saying, "I don't want to mow the lawn." A friend may be saying, "I don't like to go mall shopping." An employee may be saying to the boss, "I don't see why you gave the statements to me to file instead of Rosabel."

The *Creative Person* is a social role used by one who postures that his or her artistic talents make it "impossible" to carry out the ordinary responsibilities of life. Such an individual is so "sensitive" that other people have to carry the burden of cooking, paying bills, keeping gas in the car's tank, and remembering social obligations. Yes, there is such a thing as genuine creativity. But the reality of a creative person needs to be distinguished from the social role Creative Person. A creative person is not necessarily one who demands special consideration and special treatment. Many creative people are reasonably well

adjusted and responsible. The role of Creative Person is a fraud. Its purpose is selfish and manipulative.

You will find the above theme effectively presented in the novel *The Moon and Sixpence* by W. Somerset Maugham. The novel's central character, Charles Strickland, is based on the painter Paul Gauguin, a real person. No one denies that Paul Gauguin was genuinely creative. Working primarily during the second half of the nineteenth century, he is considered to be one of the world's great artists. As presented in the biographical novel, he used the role of Creative Person to avoid responsibility. He neglected his wife and children, and they had to be supported by her parents. He treated women like things and discarded them when he was bored with what they had to offer. His philosophy seemed to be "Everything is allowed because I have great talent."

Using the role of Creative Person is just one more way to cop out. You can be creative without playing a pretentious role.

Whining Person is a social role used by people who want to elicit pity from others. The person playing this role wants others to believe that procrastination is excusable because he or she is overburdened. Again, there is such a thing as being truly overburdened. But you can tell when someone is playing a social role because the voice becomes singsongy. The pitch goes up, making it sound as if the voice belongs to a child. The language chosen is simple and the sentences are short. Examples of Whining Person expressions include, "I have *so* much to do. I don't know how I'm going to get it all done," "I don't know why everything happens to me," "I guess I'm just unlucky or something," "That's too *hard*," and, "It just isn't *fair*."

If you are overburdened, and if someone else can help you do something about it, state the problem to the other person in realistic, not self-pitying, terms.

Tired Person is a social role frequently used by individuals in close relationships such as marriages. Postponement of responsible behavior is excusable if one is genuinely tired. As indicated in chapter 2, you can't do much if you don't have enough energy. However, genuine fatigue needs to be distinguished from deceptive fatigue. The role of Tired Person involves the flying of false colors. You convince the other person that you can't do this or that because you are too tired. And, consequently, you escape blame or criticism for your failures and shortcomings.

Although it is certainly quite tempting to use posturing social roles in order to smooth the procrastination pathway, keep in mind that these social roles are, in the long run, self-defeating. They will keep you stuck and are almost always counterproductive. If you use one or more of them, make the decision to give them up.

COPYCAT BEHAVIOR

Avoid Copycat Behavior. Copycat behavior occurs when one person uncritically imitates the behavior of another person. The desire to imitate arises from a lack of confidence in one's own judgment or an admiration of the other individual. Small-scale copycat behavior is common. Ten-year-old Jack begins to swagger and talk tough like a twelve-year-old bully who terrorizes his school. Sasha buys a carpet for her living room exactly like the one her best friend bought three months earlier.

Long-term vocational choices are sometimes made on the basis of imitation. Austin R. went to medical school and became a physician because he admired his father, a highly respected small town doctor. As a practicing physician, he was unhappy and unfulfilled. The profession did not suit his talents and interests. He began to drink heavily and abuse drugs. By the time he reached his mid-thirties he had grown to feel that the choice of medicine as a career was a great mistake. But he was having a difficult time extricating himself from it. He felt trapped.

Brett F. came from a line of military men. His father and grandfather had both been generals. Brett's father and mother frequently referred to him as a "chip off the old block." Brett was expected to carry on the family tradition, and he did. He went to West Point and graduated with honors. At first, he was a very enthusiastic officer. But ten years into his military career he was stalled. He had been passed over twice for promotion because of a lack of effectiveness and efficiency. He saw himself as a disappointment to both himself and his family.

Suzanne R. became an attorney largely because her mother was an attorney. As the daughter of a self-sufficient single mother who was often cold and dominating, Suzanne believed that she could win her mother's love and approval by imitating her behavior and becoming an attorney. It didn't work, of course. Suzanne's mother approved of Suzanne's career choice, but this didn't magically transform her into an affectionate person. Suzanne is only a fair attorney, and certainly not the efficient, well-organized person her mother is. Suzanne is, of course, regretting the poor decision she made.

Procrastination is one of the symptoms associated with making a vocational choice based on copycat behavior. At some level, even if you are only dimly aware of it, you are getting a signal that is saying, "Watch out! Think twice! Maybe you're on the wrong track."

When you follow a line of work because you admire and identify with someone else, this is not self-actualization, but *image-actualization*. Image-actualization takes place when you try to live up to an ideal associated with the admired attributes of another person, not yourself. Self-actualization takes place when you live up to your own unique talents and abilities. It is important to make a distinction between the two, or, as suggested in chapter 7, you will be running down the wrong road. If, eventually, you find yourself not running, but dragging your feet—procrastinating—it is because the motivation for copycat behavior is inherently weak.

WHOSE IDEA IS IT?

Ask Yourself, "Whose Idea Is It?" Your partner asks you to perform an unpleasant chore. Your mother calls and asks you to run an errand for her at a bad time for you. Your child asks to be driven somewhere. If you get only one or two requests a week, you probably won't have an adverse reaction. However, if the unsolicited requests start piling up, you will feel harassed. At this point, you will begin to procrastinate.

Your procrastination is rational. It is a form of protest. You have a right to ask yourself, "Whose idea is it?" If an activity or task is your own idea, you are less likely to procrastinate because the idea arises from within. It *belongs* to you. However, if an activity or task is someone else's idea, no matter how reasonable it is, the activity is, in a sense, alien to you. It is *imposed*. And we can take only so much imposed behavior. You have a right to throw up your hands and call a halt if demands are excessive.

Don't be a "nice guy" to the extent that you get used and abused. Draw a rational line. Make a distinction between requests made by loved ones that are reasonable and those that are unreasonable. Also make a distinction between an appropriate number of weekly requests and an excessively large number.

CRITICISM

Don't Be Afraid of a Criticism. I have a very sad-happy story to tell you about criticism. The story is sad because the procrastination was excessive and, ultimately, point-less. The story is happy because it had a long-run desir-able outcome.

When I was twenty years old I weighed 245 pounds. Two years later when I graduated from UCLA with a bach-elor's degree in psychology I was a normal 175 pounds. For years I dreamed of writing a book on weight control. I attributed my success to the study of psychology. So, logically, I called my book *How Psychology Can Help You Lose Weight*. I showed the first two chapters of the manuscript to a friend who, like myself, has a degree in psychology and teaches the subject. The friend read the manuscript and was very critical of it. He indicated to me that it was a hopeless effort and that I should abandon it. I took his criticism very seriously. I set the manuscript aside and ignored it for *more than five years*. Talk about procrastination!

Finally, I got a little bit of courage back and began working on the manuscript again. This time I didn't make the mistake of showing it to a friend. When I had enough material, I submitted the manuscript to a publisher. Within three weeks I had an acceptance and a contract. The book was published with the main title *Think Yourself Thin*. The subtitle is *How Psychology Can Help you Lose Weight*. It sold well as a hardcover book, and then went through fifteen paperback printings.

Since that sad experience with criticism I have learned to take criticism with a grain of salt. Much criticism is not based on a rational appraisal of your work, but on jealousy. The green-eyed monster raises its head, and your "friend" becomes sadistic.

Don't procrastinate because someone has been critical of your efforts. Heed your own counsel.

GAMES

Avoid the Blaming Game. A game, in the context of interpersonal psychology, is a power struggle in which one person "wins" and another "loses." There are quotation marks around the words *win* and *lose* to suggest that they are being used as qualified terms. The one who "wins" may have to pay a price for winning. And the same is true of the person who "loses."

These games are quite common in marriages and other close relationships. A very common game played by couples is the Blaming Game.

Caldwell and Rosalyn L. inherited a hardware store from his father early in their marriage. They worked together in the store and it thrived. Caldwell had a dominating personality and Rosalyn's was submissive. Rosalyn loved to paint and draw as a child and adolescent. She actually had quite a bit of talent and had been encouraged by art teachers and others. Rosalyn often remarked that she wanted to return to her painting and pursue an art career. If she couldn't pursue an art career, she explained to friends, she would at least like to paint as a hobby on long evenings and weekends.

Caldwell was very threatened by Rosalyn's interest in painting. He saw it as something that would take her away from him, their three children, and the frequent preparation of home-cooked meals. Consequently, he belittled her interest. When she produced a completed canvas before they had children, he did not compliment her. On the contrary, he called the painting "stupid." It was clear to Rosalyn that if she wanted Caldwell's approval, she should not paint.

On the conscious level Rosalyn wanted to paint. However, unconsciously, she resisted her talent. It threatened her. Down deep she didn't feel that she was good enough and didn't want to confront her own limitations. It was, in a sense, cozier to play along with Caldwell's wishes and dream of what she might have done than to actually work on an art project. She was avoiding looking in the mirror of the self. She was procrastinating.

Now in her midforties, Rosalyn is bitter about her lost opportunity. She frequently tells Caldwell, "If it wasn't for you I could have been a fine artist. I could have had a free-lance career with my pictures in art galleries. But, no, to you the damn hardware store and your big Sunday meals were more important." She indulges freely in her criticism. She is still in fact submissive. She works forty- to fifty-hour weeks in the hardware store and makes many home-cooked meals. But she has found her tongue and enjoys giving Caldwell lashings with it from time to time.

Rosalyn is the Loser in the Blaming Game. However, she has played the game because it allowed her to procrastinate without guilt. She could assign the fault to Caldwell's dominating personality and consequently cop out on her responsibility to herself.

Caldwell is the Winner in the Blaming Game. He gets to act superior and is superficially in charge of events. On the other hand, he has to endure Rosalyn's hostility. And he feels emotionally isolated from her.

Although the Blaming Game is defined by the Loser as "all the other person's fault," it should be noted that the real responsibility for ending the game resides with the Loser. The Winner will not stop playing the game voluntarily. The Loser has to realize that the game is a kind of self-indulgence, bringing a psychological benefit of sorts. And it provides a handy excuse for procrastination. Additionally, the Loser pays the higher price for playing the Blaming Game. Consequently it is up to the person in the losing position to call his or her own bluff as well as the bluff of the other person. The Loser has to act in an assertive manner and execute realistic actions that will end the game.

The Loser in the Blaming Game plays the game out of the child self. He or she has to recognize that it is always possible to voluntarily move into the adult self and act in an effective, responsible manner.

It is not too late for Rosalyn. She is forty-two years old, still young enough to accomplish a lot. But she has to look to herself to stop the self-defeating Blaming Game, not Caldwell.

The Blaming Game's details vary from couple to couple. And the game also appears frequently in parent-child relationships and in friendships. But the basic outlines of the game remain the same. The person who plays the part of Loser is using this game position as a way of avoiding self-confrontation. It is a way of running away from a psychological threat. For all of its irritation, the Blaming Game is a kind of security blanket.

If you are playing the Blaming Game, no matter how long you have played it, it is important to reclaim your personal freedom. A game takes two. Like a dance, it "takes two to tango." If you decide to stop dancing, the dance will end. If you decide to stop playing, the game will end.

The Last Word

If a tendency on your part toward chronic procrastination is being aggravated by the actions of another person, it is important for you to realize that you have a real choice in the matter. Other people have no real power over us unless we grant it to them. When you find yourself feeling used and abused, it is time to take stock and make a conscious decision to stop playing the social role of Victim.

Don't allow yourself to be manipulated. Decide what you want and need to do, and *do it*. In this way you will take charge of your life and your time. Effectively managing time in your own way is an important key that unlocks the door confining you to the prison of procrastination.

Key Points to Remember

□—	*Interpersonal behavior* is behavior that involves interactions with other people.

□—	The *interpersonal stimulus* is manifest when you make an attempt to elicit a response from someone else. The *interpersonal response* is manifest when the other person reacts to the stimulus you presented.

□—	The *interpersonal interaction* is the living pattern created by the stimulus and response.

□—	Reject the temptation to be passive.

□—	Play by the boss's rules.

□—	Avoid posturing social roles. Examples of such roles include the Slowpoke, the Creative Person, the Whining Person, and the Tired Person.

□—	Avoid copycat behavior.

□—	*Image-actualization* is not self-actualization.

□—	Ask yourself, "Whose idea is it?"

□—	Don't be afraid of criticism.

□—	Avoid the Blaming Game.

9 BECOMING A DOER: THE POWER OF POSITIVE ACTION

The Adventures of Pinocchio was written by Carlo Lorenzini and published in Italy in 1883. Millions of children and adults have seen the movie versions of the story. Pinocchio is a puppet who yearns to become a real boy and eventually succeeds. On the surface, the story seems to be merely an entertaining fantasy. After all, a puppet can't become a person.

However, at a deeper level, the story is a powerful metaphor for life. A puppet is a thing. Its strings are pulled by others, and its source of motion is *external*. A person is a living being who can, so to speak, pull his or her own strings. The source of motion is *internal*.

Like Pinocchio, we find ourselves and become truly alive when we determine our own behavior from within.

A formal distinction can be made between reactive behavior and proactive behavior. *Reactive behavior* is a familiar term. It takes place when an external stimulus elicits a response or otherwise goads you into action. *Proactive behavior* is a less familiar term. It takes place when you will your own behavior, when the self is the source of action.

If most of your behavior is reactive, you are somewhat like a puppet. You are *acted upon*, but you don't initiate action. If most of your behavior is proactive, then you are exhibiting an attribute that is associated with being fully alive.

Taking Charge

The self-directed strategies presented in this book have all been designed to help you to become more proactive, more able to take charge of your own time and behavior. This section provides a final set of tips that will help you consolidate your proactive resources and help you stop procrastinating.

POSITIVE ACTION

Remember That Positive Action Is More Powerful Than Positive Thought. We hear a lot about the power of positive thinking. And positive thinking is certainly important. The thought, after all, is the parent of the deed. Nonetheless, it is important to shift your focus from thinking to *action*. Here is a little experiment: Place your hand on the surface of a table. Now think about raising your index finger while holding the rest of your hand stationary. I assume you have a mental picture of your finger moving. But it is not *actually* moving. Why? Because you are just *thinking*, not acting.

Now follow a second set of instructions: Lift your index finger. Now the finger is actually moving. What's the difference? In the case of the second set of instructions you used the power of will to induce action.

You won't do anything if you don't bring a certain amount of will into play. First, you think. Second, you will. Third, you act. Keep this sequence in mind. Positive thought is necessary, but not sufficient. Will supplies the all-important link between thought and action. Until thought is converted into action, it is just useless mental steam.

WHEEL SPINNING

Stop Spinning Your Wheels. In connection with the prior observations, stop spinning your wheels. From a psychological standpoint this means stop preparing, preparing, preparing. One of the common characteristics of people who suffer from chronic procrastination is that they either gather too much information or spend too much time getting ready. This saps their mental energy to such an extent that they haven't got much left over for the actual task. Meanwhile the doing, the action, gets delayed and delayed. Sometimes it never gets done.

Edgar and Nora D., an affluent couple in their late forties, yearn to build their dream house. They have talked to architects, looked at lots, bought books of house plans, spoken to building contractors, and so forth. All wise activities, you say? True. The only problem is that Edgar and Nora have been doing this for more than five years. They are hopelessly confused. They are so bogged down in contradictory information that it will be a wonder if the dream house ever gets built.

Here is good advice for Edgar and Nora: Set everything aside. Don't give any more conscious thought to the gathering of information. Don't talk about the pros and cons of anything for a while. The time for preparation is over. Allow for a quiet incubation period. At a certain point a more or less favorable approach to making a decision will emerge. At this point it is time to act without looking backwards.

Louis O., a high school English teacher, wants to write a novel. He wants it to be a commercial, blockbuster best-seller. He reads best-sellers and calls them "best-smellers." He tells his wife that he can easily do far better. He has read twenty different books on how to write novels and how to write for money. He has taken graduate courses on the subject. He has outlined ten different plots. He has read many contemporary novels. He has also read the classics. He is completely stalled. He is *too* informed. He is overwhelmed by all the factors he thinks he must juggle to pull off a successful novel. He still maintains his brave front with his wife, but he can't cut through the tangle of information he has acquired. In fact, he's acquired so much information that it has become disinformation. And he hasn't written an actual line of a novel.

Again, it is time to allow for an incubation period. Louis should stop gathering information and set everything aside for a while. Then at a certain point he will feel ready to act. He will be able to get to work without too much analysis and reflection, and he'll get something done.

SPONTANEITY

Reclaim Your Spontaneity. To do something spontaneously means to do it without too much self-analysis and self-criticism. Spontaneous behavior takes place with a minimum of planning and a maximum of joy. It is an essential ingredient in the creative process.

There is a great misunderstanding about spontaneity. It seems to many people that spontaneous behavior is impulsive and irresponsible. Nothing could be farther from the truth. Let's examine a common experience, one that many people have had: taking music lessons. Marcy is three years old. She loves to bang on the piano in the living room. Her parents believe that she likes to do this more than most children. They ask her, "Would you like to take music lessons when you get older?" They are rewarded with an enthusiastic, "Yes!"

Is Marcy's banging spontaneous behavior? No, it's *impulsive behavior* because there is no thoughtful or creative content to it at all. It is just the totally unreflective, unplanned behavior of the preschooler.

Now let's look in on Marcy at the age of eight. She is taking music lessons from an authoritarian piano teacher who insists that Marcy practice her scales and play songs exactly as written. The songs are exercises without words, and Marcy finds them unbelievably tedious. Nonetheless, she sticks with the lessons and practices because she really does have an interest in learning to play the piano. However, Marcy plays in a stiff, mechanical fashion. All of the impulsive behavior is gone. It has been replaced by a robotlike performance. When asked to play a piece for a visiting relative from another state, Marcy is self-conscious. She starts playing, makes a mistake, and says in an apologetic voice, "Let me start over." Her present way of playing the piano can be described as *compulsive*.

Let's fast forward our time tape to Marcy at age sixteen. Now she is taking piano lessons from a man who used to have a small dance band. He is an expert at improvisation and plays all of the popular standards, the blues, jazz, rock 'n' roll, and even old-fashioned boogie-woogie. He teaches Marcy harmony and the ways in which chords can be constructed and inverted. He shows her how one can follow the rules of music and still perform with a lot of playful freedom.

Our final visit with Marcy is at age twenty-five. She seldom plays a song in the same way twice, always exploring new ways to present old material. She often writes and performs her own melodies. In short, her behavior has become *spontaneous*. Note that the natural progression of Marcy's learning, and of much learning, has been from impulsive to compulsive to spontaneous. Impulsive behavior and compulsive behavior reside at opposite ends of a psychological pole. Spontaneous behavior is the hybrid, the happy medium that brings the two together in such a way as to form a higher synthesis.

Spontaneous behavior is natural to human beings. But it is often sacrificed on the altar of self-analysis, overtraining, and perfectionism. There is nothing irresponsible about spontaneity. On the contrary, it is a healthy, open expression of a fully functioning mind. In his studies of self-actualizing persons, Abraham Maslow found it to be one of their prime characteristics.

STARTING AND STOPPING

Know How to Start and Know When to Stop. Much of this book has focused on getting yourself started, on *not* procrastinating. However, in chapter 6 I made reference to the problem of violating your own behavioral contract. If you have overcome resistance to getting started by defining a task in a limited way, your child self will feel betrayed if you keep working on and on. You may get away with this kind of behavior for awhile. You may think that because you've got a momentum going you should take advantage of it. Often it *is* as hard to stop as it is to get started.

But don't deceive yourself. If you overshoot in this way, when you try to make another start on a similar task, you will experience great inner resistance. Your child self says, "No way am I going to make a deal with you. You don't live up to your end of the bargain!" And you may very well find yourself returning to the habit of procrastination.

PACING

Learn to Pace Yourself. Take a lesson from the behavior of the tortoise in the fable of the tortoise and the hare. The hare could have easily won the race, but he lost it because he procrastinated. He procrastinated because the task was so *easy*. He disdained the task required to win the race (running). For the tortoise, the task was difficult. So he plodded along, moving slowly, but steadily, toward his goal. And he won the race while the hare was napping.

This is a fable for all of us. You may find a task so easy or so "beneath my talents" that you take your sweet time getting to it. Meanwhile, someone with less talent, but more persistence, bests you. Don't let this happen. Learn to pace yourself. Start early and work along steadily, and, like the tortoise, you will be the winner in the long run.

FIVE MINUTES

Realize That Even Five Minutes Is Real Time. It is common to hear people complain that they don't have time available to do this or that. The fact is that we often have small bits of uncommitted time available. For example, you may be ready to go to work in the morning five minutes before your normal departure time. If you define five minutes as zero time, then you have no time. On the other hand, if you define five minutes as a block of finite time, you can get something done.

Using a five-minute segment, it is possible to do one of these things: pay a bill, write a thank-you note, make a bed, floss your teeth, throw out a container of trash, or drop a letter in a mailbox. None of this suggests that you should be doing things at a frantic, nervous pace. Again, look to the tortoise. You should realize that even five minutes is not zero time, that even five minutes can be employed as a functional period to help you stop procrastinating.

TALKING

Don't Overtalk Your Ideas. You've got an idea. You think that it's a fairly good one. It inspires you to make some plans. You tell a friend your ideas and your plans. Let's say that your friend is not critical, but supportive. Your friend says, "That's great! Get started." (I have already warned about the risks of negative criticism.) You tell someone else. Again you get encouragement. Oh, boy! This is going great! You're having great fun. You're getting a lot of approval and recognition. You tell someone else.

Six months later the first friend you talked to asks, "What about that great idea of yours? Did you go ahead and do the things you were talking about? How's it going?"

A sad look comes over your face. "Oh, I haven't gotten started yet. But I will."

"What went wrong? You were so enthusiastic."

"Yeah. I know. I don't know what went wrong. I just—."

You just what? You just took all of the wind out of your sails by overtalking your idea and your plans. You got so much encouragement for palaver that it robbed you of much of the need for action. We act to a large extent in order to earn recognition. If we can get the same recognition cheaply by empty talk instead of action, we may not act at all.

So don't take the wind out of your own sails by overtalking your ideas. Conserve the psychological energy associated with them. The things you want to do that are really important to you should remain to a large extent within your private psychological and emotional domain.

WHEN?

Ask Yourself, "If Not Now, When?" This question is one of the great questions posed by Hillel the Elder, a Jewish rabbi and famous teacher who lived approximately two thousand years ago. It is a question meant to be posed to oneself. In most cases, asking yourself the question will alert your mind to the fact that time is slipping away, that indeed, there really is no time like the present. Recognition of the validity of your own mental response will help you to actually start taking effective action.

MR. MEANT-TO

Return to Mr. Meant-To. You will find the poem "Mr. Meant-To" in chapter 7. I suggested that you memorize it. I hope you didn't procrastinate and say, "I'll memorize it later." Perhaps it has already entered and exited your short-term memory. If so, return to it now and actually memorize it. Rehearse it until you know it cold. Then when you feel tempted to procrastinate, recite the poem mentally, and you will find that it will have a wonderful transforming and motivating effect. It should be one of the principal psychological weapons in your fight against procrastination.

THE MOVING FINGER

Remember the Moving Finger. The Rubáiyát of Omar Khayyám was written by the eleventh century Persian poet, astronomer, and mathematician Omar Khayyám. It was translated into English by Edward FitzGerald. The title is derived from the Arabic *rubai*, meaning "quatrain," or four-line verse. One of the most powerful quatrains from the Rubáiyát is this one:

> *The Moving Finger writes; and having writ,*
> *Moves on: nor all thy Piety nor Wit*
> *Shall lure it back to cancel half a line,*
> *Nor all thy Tears wash out a Word of it.*

The moving finger can be thought of as the finger of time. The quatrain suggests that we are the authors of our own destiny, that we have to live all of our lives with the consequences of our decisions and actions. It also implies that time should not be wasted because a neglected opportunity may not present itself again. You may not get a second chance.

The Last Word

Make the phrase *carpe diem* an important part of your philosophy of life. The phrase is Latin for "seize the day." It can be traced back approximately twenty centuries to the writings of the Roman poet Horace. The two words received renewed popularity when they were presented in the 1989 motion picture *Dead Poets Society*. A literature teacher played by Robin Williams tells a group of students "*Carpe diem*" in order to impress upon them the importance of using time wisely and constructively in order to make the most of one's life at all levels.

God or Nature gave you this day to work or love or play. Use the day wisely. Stop procrastinating.

Carpe diem.

Seize the day.

Key Points to Remember

□— Reactive behavior takes place when an external stimulus elicits a response or otherwise goads you into action.

□— Proactive behavior takes place when you will your own behavior, when the self is the source of action.

□— Remember that positive action is more powerful than positive thought.

□— Stop spinning your wheels.

□— Reclaim your spontaneity.

□— Know how to start and know when to stop.

□— Learn to pace yourself.

□— Realize that even five minutes is real time.

□— Don't overtalk your ideas.

□— Ask yourself, "If not now, when?"

□— Return to "Mr. Meant-To."

□— Remember the moving finger.

□— Make the phrase *carpe diem*, meaning "seize the day," an important part of your philosophy of life.

10 A NINE-STEP ANTI-PROCRASTINATION PROGRAM

Perhaps you have already made a good start in your effort to defeat chronic procrastination. I hope you have been applying some of the suggestions in the book as you went along.

On the other hand, it is possible to feel stalled. Perhaps you don't know where or how to start. As one person said, "I keep procrastinating about starting to stop procrastinating."

This chapter is designed to help you sort things out, to simplify, and to actually get you going on an anti-procrastination program.

The Weakest Link Approach

Remember this principle: Any start at all is better than no start. In a prior chapter I advised, in some cases, to make a half-baked start. So if you want to, just follow your nose. Your intuition will almost certainly lead you to the self-directed strategy that you need *now*, one that breaks the weakest link in the chronic procrastination chain. By breaking the weakest link you are well on your way to destroying the whole chain.

So one approach to overcoming chronic procrastination is to act on any suggestion that appeals to you. Make it work, and then move on to another suggestion. This seemingly random approach to your problem can be very effective. Actually, it is not random at all. It is subconsciously determined by your own needs and motivational structure.

The Nine-Step Program

On the other hand, you might want to be systematic. <u>You seek to slay the procrastination dragon piece by piece in an orderly fashion.</u>

I have designed the book in such a way that each chapter precedes the subsequent one in a logical fashion. The material builds upon itself like a series of ascending steps. And you can proceed one logical step at a time. If this approach appeals to you, here are the nine steps.

STEP 1

Turn to chapter 2, "Fatigue and Delay." Ask yourself if genuine fatigue is an important factor in your tendency to procrastinate. If the answer is yes, then make the overcoming of fatigue your first priority. Find the section headed "Boosting Your Energy Level," and survey its suggestions. Pick one that seems particularly important and put it to work. Continue in this manner until you are convinced that fatigue is not what is stopping you from more effective behavior.

On the other hand, if fatigue does not appear to play an important part in your tendency to procrastinate, skip the applications in this chapter, and go directly to chapter 3.

STEP 2

Turn to chapter 3, "Resistance." This chapter is designed to help you understand your own internal barriers to effective action. It gives you insight into how you place blocks in your own pathway. And it shows you how to remove these blocks.

Find the section headed "Overcoming Resistance." Evaluate the self-directed strategies, and apply one that seems particularly important to you. Work on this for one week. You do not have to feel that you have attained complete success before you move on. However, don't try to use all of the suggestions simultaneously. Just select one.

STEP 3

Turn to chapter 4, "Stop Kidding Yourself." This chapter is designed to help you avoid the excessive use of self-deceiving ego defense mechanisms. Ego defense mechanisms are the ways in which the conscious self protects itself against threats to its integrity.

Turn to the section headed "Avoiding Defense Mechanisms." Select a strategy in accordance with the instructions given in Step 2. Follow the same procedure outlined in Step 2. After one week of application, go to Step 4.

STEP 4

Turn to chapter 5, "Subduing an Inferiority Complex." The aim of this chapter is to help you turn a psychological minus into a plus. Feelings of inadequacy often play an important role in chronic procrastination. It is difficult to move forward if you have doubts about your capacity to do so.

Find the heading with the same title as the chapter, "Subduing an Inferiority Complex." Select a strategy in accordance with procedure described in Step 2. After a week of application, go to Step 5.

STEP 5

Turn to chapter 6, "Nobody Is a Born Procrastinator." This chapter approaches chronic procrastination as a habit to be broken or modified. A habit is learned, and what has been learned can be unlearned. In this viewpoint, there is hope.

Find the section "Breaking Out." Make a habit analysis in accordance with the chapter's instructions. Work on one of your specific procrastination habits for about one week, then move on to Step 6.

STEP 6

Turn to chapter 7, "Reaching Your Goals and Dreams." This chapter asserts that one of the best ways to avoid procrastination is to ask yourself: "Where am I going?" Its important theme is stated in the subtitle: "What Is the Use of Running If You're on the Wrong Road?"

Find the section headed "Making Practical Applications." Select a strategy in accordance with the procedure described in Step 2. After a week of work, go to Step 7.

STEP 7

Turn to chapter 8, "Interpersonal Aspects." This chapter is based on the assumption that your relationships with other people often have much to do with your tendency to procrastinate. Self-defeating games and power struggles interfere with constructive action.

Find the section headed "Coping Strategies." Select a strategy in accordance with the procedure described in Step 2. After a week of application, go to Step 8.

STEP 8

Turn to chapter 9, "Becoming a Doer." Chapter 9 makes a distinction between reactive behavior and proactive behavior. A set of final tips are presented that will help you to discover your capacity for proactive behavior.

Find the section headed "Taking Charge." Select a strategy that has strong appeal to you. After a week of application, go to Step 9.

STEP 9

Give yourself a one-week break. Don't work consciously on stopping procrastination. Of course, after approximately eight weeks of work, you have probably acquired some new behavioral tendencies. Perhaps you have licked the problem to your satisfaction. If so, great! Put the book aside and get on with your life.

On the other hand, you may perceive that there has been a lot of improvement in your behavior, but there is still some work to be done. Then repeat the program.

Learning to stop procrastinating is just that, *learning*. Fortunately, there is a phenomenon well known in psychology called *learning to learn*. When we learn, we not only learn a specific fact, concept, skill, or habit, we also become better learners. What this means in the case of the anti-procrastination program is that every time you go over it, the learning becomes easier and easier. Success often resides in a willingness to persist and repeat.

Repetition will make you a master of the self-directed strategies presented in the book.

The Last Word

Keep *Stop Procrastinating* in a handy place. When you feel yourself tempted in the direction of unnecessary procrastination, turn to it as you would to a helpful friend.

Think of your waking moments in each twenty-four-hour cycle as magnificent opportunities to work, to play, or to love.

Again, make the words *carpe diem* an important part of your philosophy of life. Seize the day.

Key Points to Remember

□— This chapter presented two alternative approaches designed to help you stop procrastinating.

□— The first alternative is the *weakest link approach*. Using this approach, you follow your intuition and subconscious inclinations.

□— The second alternative is systematic. It is the *nine-step anti-procrastination program* outlined in the chapter.